FRESH
Oil

FRESH *Oil*

CHRIS GARCIA

CHARISMA
HOUSE

FRESH OIL by Chris Garcia
Published by Charisma House, an imprint of Charisma
Media
1150 Greenwood Blvd., Lake Mary, Florida 32746

For more resources like this, visit MyCharismaShop.com and the author's website at www.fathersglory.org.

Cataloging-in-Publication Data is on file with the Library of Congress.
International Standard Book Number: 978-1-63641-395-2
E-book ISBN: 978-1-63641-396-9

1 2024
Printed in the United States of America

Most Charisma Media products are available at special quantity discounts for bulk purchase for sales promotions, premiums, fund-raising, and educational needs. For details, call us at (407) 333-0600 or visit our website at www.charismamedia.com.

DEDICATION

THIS BOOK IS dedicated to you, the reader—to those who love the Lord but desire to get to know Him with greater awareness. It is written to you who are not sure where to start your spiritual walk or how to even begin to pray and make the secret place your dwelling place.

This book is dedicated to all who wish to learn how to access this new and living way—our intimacy with the Holy Spirit that is provided joyfully and liberally by the gospel. To those who see prayer as daunting and even intimidating, yes, this is for you! For the moms who are juggling and bustling through children's appointments and kids' events, this is for you.

For new, zealous lovers of God who feel stuck in their ruts and strivings and want to learn to operate from a place of rest, this is for you too! For the spiritually mature who need a fresh reminder of the Spirit's renewal, yes, this is for you too!

For anyone in any stage of life and spiritual development, this is all for you! This book is dedicated to all who want to tap into fresh oil and greater intimate depths of the Spirit.

This book is also especially dedicated to my beautiful, loving wife, Zuly, who is my dearest friend and companion, and my three children: Yadiel, Zoey, and David, in whom I take great delight.

CONTENTS

HAVE YOU BEEN THERE?

THERE WAS A time in my life when I was so very close to God. As a young teenager, I had extraordinary visitations from the Holy Spirit, and praying was as easy as breathing. I felt such peace and refreshment in my life with the Lord. I would spend hours on end reading and meditating on the Word of God, praying in the Spirit, and worshipping in the presence of Christ. Passion for God raged like a fire deep within my being. Love for God, the lost, and the church were the beat of my heart. But slowly I grew distracted and careless in my walk with the Lord, and I stumbled often, yielding to fleshly impulses and creating strongholds. The complacent, lukewarm waters of life began to quench the fire that once consumed me. This resulted in a ten-year dry season.

I used to pray, "God, bring me back to the place where I once was! I want to go back to where I was!" My cries often were met with silence, and frustration would well up within me. Proverbs 13:12 (NIV) says, "Hope deferred makes the heart sick," and that is how I felt. Through all my praying, the only thing that kept coming to me was to be faithful in the wilderness and that this was only temporary. I didn't realize it at the time, but God had no desire to "bring me back." He wanted me to go beyond my past experiences into greater glory.

I still loved God, served Him, and even ministered, but my heart was like a bag of dust. I so desperately needed refreshing. Sometimes, even while serving God, you can forget Him. You can preach about Him without ever being with Him. You can minister to God's people without ever ministering to Him directly. I have been there. The vast majority of believers are stuck in this state. They have just enough of God to make them miserable with their sin and just enough of the world to make them apathetic to the things of God. In this dry season the Spirit taught me to remember Him. It's easy to forget the Lord when you have lost fellowship with Him. But once you regain it, you are flooded with the familiar embraces of His life-giving presence.

THE FIRST DRAW

Jesus said, "No one can come to Me unless the Father who sent Me draws him" (John 6:44). This is entirely true, but once we come to faith in Christ, there are times when we must take a step toward Him before we'll sense Him drawing near to us. I call this the first draw. Why would God require that? It is because He "has given to us all things that pertain to life and godliness" (2 Pet. 1:3, MEV). He has already given us all we need to get close to Him. We just need to agree with Him and draw near in faith.

The Scriptures say, "But now in Christ Jesus you who once were far off have been brought near by the blood of Christ" (Eph. 2:13). You see, Jesus' blood, His atoning sacrifice, has already brought us near to Him. We just need to believe this and walk in that reality. Too often we are led by our souls and our carnal thoughts and feelings, but our feelings do not dictate truth—God's Word does. Our minds will disqualify and accuse us before we receive from God because a carnal mind is at enmity with God. An unrenewed mind is a carnal, natural mind that automatically opposes the truth of God's Word. When you begin to think you're excluded from God's presence, remember that those thoughts are lies opposing the goodness of God in your life.

The apostle James rebuked the believers for being double-minded and fleshly, saying,

> Do you not know that friendship with the world is enmity with God? Whoever therefore

wants to be a friend of the world makes himself an enemy of God.

—JAMES 4:4

Then he presents the solution:

Draw near to God and He will draw near to you. Cleanse your hands, you sinners; and purify your hearts, you double-minded.... Humble yourselves in the sight of the Lord, and He will lift you up.

—JAMES 4:8, 10

Notice that we need to draw near and enter into a time of repentance *first*. Then He lifts us up.

When we are dealing with the effect of sin and being fleshly minded, it is very difficult for us to draw near because our minds are set on the lies birthed by the carnal nature. Yet despite the difficulty, there are times in life when we have to draw near to Him first. There are a variety of reasons for this. You may be in a time of transition, or perhaps you are about to enter a new degree of God's glory. Whatever the reason, there are times when you must make the first draw.

Do you feel distant? Draw near. Do you long for refreshment? Draw near! Throw yourself at His feet. Sometimes that drawing requires patience and trust. But if you do your part, He will do His part. He can be trusted!

Sometimes repentance is needed before we can draw near because it's easy to stray into our own works and depend on our own strengths. That disposition of the heart is called pride, and "God resists the proud, but gives grace to the humble" (Jas. 4:6). Humility is when you rely on and adore Him, acknowledging your need for Him. When you take that posture, God will bring you to Himself. The more you rely on Him alone, the more He releases His grace to you.

You will never, on this side of heaven, arrive at absolute perfection, so there will always be times when you need to make the first draw. If you can learn this key, you will see spiritual lulls as invitations to draw near and go deeper in Him.

SOWING TO PLEASE THE SPIRIT

In 2015, at about 5 a.m., I got up to spend some time alone with the Lord in our small apartment. It was in this season that I recall very strong manifestations of God's presence. These times with God were tangible and overwhelming.

This particular morning I sought God but did not sense or feel a thing. I began to grow frustrated. I felt like a deer panting after water. I remember crying out to the Lord and doing what I call spiritual gymnastics: I started begging, screaming, and trying to twist God's arm to get Him to move. You can't do this with God. You'll be moving in fleshly performance, not grace.

Well, on that early morning, I tried everything I knew to get God to speak, and I remember feeling so very tired. I said, "God, if Your presence is not with me, I don't want to pray. I can't pray!" I was thinking He might do or say something in response. My heart felt so dry; I just wanted to feel His presence. But I got no response—nothing! I eventually stopped my pleading and religious acrobatics, took a shower, and got ready for work. Still in a frustrated and irritated frenzy, I remember being on the verge of tears. I thought God would be impressed with me for getting up early to seek Him, but now I felt I had wasted my time.

As I ran down the stairs, I began to grow angrier and angrier at God. It felt as if He had left me. But when I got into my car and started the engine, the presence of the Holy Spirit flooded my vehicle. Tears of joy and surprise welled up, and I said, "Lord! What are You doing here?" His reply forever changed the way I prayed. He spoke to me so clearly and said, "They that sow to the flesh will from the flesh reap death and corruption, but they that sow to please the Spirit will from the Spirit reap life everlasting. Chris, if you live to sow to what pleases Me, if you spend time with Me, it doesn't matter if you feel Me or do not feel Me. You are sowing to please Me, and you will reap My life and presence throughout your day."

When God spoke, it felt as if my whole being received it in layers, as if I was hearing Him from various directions all at once. I immediately understood what He was saying. He was teaching me that my time with Him could not be based on how I felt. It did not revolve around me and what I wanted to get from the Lord. It was about pleasing Him and giving Him glory because He is worthy. It was about knowing that even if I don't feel Him, He is with me.

Feelings come and go. They can be carnal at times and hinder greater intimate, Spirit-to-spirit connection. I based my walk with God on what I felt, but the Lord showed me that when I felt His nearness, He was with me, and when I did not perceive Him, He was still with me. From that point on, I did not pray to feel God; I prayed to please Him. As I adjusted my heart, I easily perceived His presence throughout my day. By loving Him for who He is, a greater sensitivity to God's Spirit was birthed in me.

SEEK HIS FACE

Many times we approach God trying to get something from His hands when He wants us to seek His face. When we seek His face out of a desire to draw near to Him, we will find ourselves receiving from His hands. It's all about the posture of our hearts.

Our desire to feel God's presence can overpower the gentle blowing of His Spirit. A marriage isn't based just on physical intimacy and emotional connections; rather, it grows through the deep, intimate time couples spend together connecting. Touch and pleasure naturally flow out of that intimacy. God wants you to feel His nearness, but even more than that, He wants you to grow in deeper intimacy with Him—intimacy that comes from knowing and believing Him.

It is faith that He is after. We must not be moved by what we see or feel but by whom we believe in. When you desire to know God, you will gain everything that comes with knowing Him. Intimacy is incubated in the womb of daily, consistent fellowship with God. The door is faith in God—believing "that He is, and that He is a rewarder of those who diligently seek Him" (Heb. 11:6). Draw near even when you don't sense Him right away. If you sow to what pleases Him simply because He is worthy, you will reap of His life and presence throughout your day!

I want to remind you that intimacy with the Spirit of God is spiritual, not mechanical. This book is not some intellectual treatise on the mechanics of prayer and growing in your relationship with God. Rather, my prayer is that this book will be a tool for impartation, a spark from the heart of God into yours, igniting the embers of first love. The eight secrets I share in this book will show you not only how to draw near but also how to stay near. It will help you make communion with God a natural part of your life so you can reap all the benefits of knowing Him.

Some of the most powerful, intimate moments of our lives are beyond human understanding and logic. They are beyond words. Our relationship with God is often like that. The beauty of God's presence and glory cannot be described or understood from a natural perspective, as if we could figure Him out. Rather, the beauty of God's presence and glory is to be tasted and seen. It is to be experienced. It is my hope that by writing this book, I can share this experience with you—the experience of knowing God personally!

Toward the end of his life, the apostle John wrote, "That...which we have seen with our eyes, which we have looked upon, and our hands have handled, concerning the Word of life...that which we have seen and heard we declare to you" (1 John 1:1, 3). That is what this book is—an invitation to experience the One I've come to know and love.

Jesus is the One who is anointed with the oil of gladness, the oil of bliss. Allow Him to anoint you with His fresh oil! The reality is that there are no secrets. When we live in the secret place, there we will hear Him speak and sense His touch. There we will see Him as He truly is and be changed into His glorious image by His Spirit.

May the fresh oil of God's Spirit give you eyes to see Him. And may the joy of your salvation and the simplicity of knowing the Lord revive and restore your hungry heart.

Before we go on, let's pray:

> *Heavenly Father, I pray that by Your Spirit You would enliven us. Help us understand how to walk in the Spirit. Help us know the difference between our emotional self and our spiritual self. May our lives be dominated by the Spirit and bring us into deep fellowship with You. Give us a yearning to live in consecration, obedience, and close relationship with You.*
>
> *Lord, unveil the Scripture to us. Be our teacher and guide. Teach us, show us, and reveal to us what we have been given in You. Your Word is alive and powerful. It's "sharper than any two-edged sword, piercing even to the division of soul and spirit, and of joints and marrow, and is a discerner of the thoughts and intents of the heart" (Heb. 4:12). By Your Word were the worlds formed. By Your Word all things were*

created and we are renewed in the spirit of our minds.

Unveil Jesus to us. Unveil the Father to us. Unveil the Spirit to us that we may glorify You all the days of our lives on earth and thereafter. In Jesus' name, amen.

Chapter 1

THE FIRST SECRET:
THE SECRET PLACE

WHAT MADE JESUS' ministry so powerful wasn't just the signs, wonders, and miracles He performed. It wasn't just His ability to preach and teach with authority. It wasn't just His ability to cast out devils and raise the dead. Yes, all those things were absolutely extraordinary. Jesus was marvelously endowed with power from the Holy Spirit, but that wasn't the only thing that fueled His public ministry. Jesus lived and dwelled in the secret place.

Scripture shows us that Jesus often went to a solitary place to pray.

> And when He had sent the multitudes away, He went up on the mountain by Himself to pray.
> —MATTHEW 14:23

> Now in the morning, having risen a long while before daylight, He went out and departed to a solitary place; and there He prayed.
>
> —MARK 1:35

> He Himself often withdrew into the wilderness and prayed.
>
> —LUKE 5:16

> Now it came to pass in those days that He went out to the mountain to pray, and continued all night in prayer to God.
>
> —LUKE 6:12

I find it interesting that in Luke 11:1, after the disciples had followed Jesus around for a while and had seen the miracles and signs of His power, they asked Him to teach them how to pray. The disciples recognized that Jesus' public ministry was marked by intimate prayer, and they wanted to understand what made Jesus' prayer life different from what they previously had seen and been taught.

When Jesus explained how to pray, He told His disciples:

> And when you pray, you shall not be like the hypocrites. For they love to pray standing in the synagogues and on the corners of the streets, that they may be seen by men. Assuredly, I say to you, they have their reward. But you, when you pray, go into your room, and when you

have shut your door, pray to your Father who is in the secret place; and your Father who sees in secret will reward you openly.

—MATTHEW 6:5–6

One of the most important doors that unlocks deep intimacy with the Holy Spirit is valuing the secret place. This is the foundation for deep communion with God. As its name implies, the secret place is not a public space. It is where no one sees. There are no cheers or applause, no outside voices or opinions. There is only an audience of One.

Why is the secret place so important to the Holy Spirit? Because He wants to exchange His thoughts and His very heart with you from that place. In the secret place there are no hindrances or distractions because it is only Him and you. In secret places, where no one sees, your true thoughts and heart are revealed because there is no facade, no masks, and no acting. In that place there is full transparency, and the motives and intent of the heart are exposed.

The deepest part of God wants to touch the deepest part of you. The Spirit of God is attracted to a heart that is laid bare before Him because God is truth, and those who go to Him "must worship in spirit and truth" (John 4:24)!

The sin of the Pharisees wasn't their piety but their hidden motives and desires to be seen and praised by man. They were enthralled with public affirmations and denounced by Jesus because of their secret intentions. God does not see the way man does. "Man looks on the outward appearance, but [it is God who] looks on the heart" (1 Sam. 16:7, MEV). God sees what is secret because He lives in the realm of the secret.

Some of the most profound moments in the human experience are times of secret intimacy. The deepest connection a husband can have with his wife happens behind closed doors. One of my favorite things to do after I spend some time in prayer is spend time with my wife. We have this special thing we do each morning. It's not something mechanical or from a place of obligation but from pure love and relationship. It's unrehearsed and happens just because we are alone in the same room. Often after prayer we meet in our kitchen with coffee in our hands and simply gaze at each other. That simple act cascades into feelings of joy and love, and without even thinking about it, we embrace each other as we continue to lock eyes.

We don't really say much; we're just present in the moment. That is our time just before the kids wake up. It is our secret place as a couple, and we find refreshment in each other's presence. Many memories are made in that place. New embraces and kisses take place there. Peace in our marriage happens there.

That place is not reserved for the public eye. In much the same way, the deepest spiritual connection happens in the place where no one sees except you and God. This is where true intimacy with the Holy Spirit is birthed. It is where sensitivity to the Holy Spirit begins.

The Holy Spirit is waiting for you in the secret place. When a couple's intimacy in the secret place leads to conception, it eventually becomes apparent that the wife is pregnant by her glowing skin and full womb. So it is with you! Your intimate moments in the secret place will cause you to conceive of God's Spirit and to come out glowing and full of His life within you. What you do in secret will soon become evident in the public space, and others will see the fullness of the Holy Spirit's touch in you. That will be the Father "rewarding you openly."

DWELLING IN SECRET

Many people want a mighty visitation from the Lord, and that is a wonderful desire to have. But what if I told you it is possible to go from a visitation to a habitation of the Holy Spirit and be marked by His presence in you and on you? That habitation is found by prioritizing and dwelling in the secret place.

Psalm 91:1 declares, "He who dwells in the secret place of the Most High shall abide under the shadow of the Almighty." This reveals what life in the secret place looks like. It is habitually making God's presence your home. Dwelling in the secret place will cause you to abide in the shelter of His presence.

JEALOUSLY GUARD THE SECRET PLACE, FOR THAT IS WHERE GOD DWELLS!

What are you dwelling in? Are you dwelling in your fears and frustrations? Are you dwelling in your past and shortcomings? Are you dwelling in your insecurities and doubts? All such frailties and limitations melt away when you choose to dwell in the secret place.

To cultivate intimacy with the Holy Spirit, your priority should be to set aside intentional time to be in the secret place. The secret place is any space where you spend time with God in secret. Your living room can turn into a palace for His presence. Your bathroom floor can become a sea of glass (Rev. 4:6), and your closet can transform into a prayer chamber.

Prioritize making your aim the secret place. In an age of distractions, nearly everything is designed to pull you away from spending time in the secret place. Jealously guard the secret place, for that is where God dwells!

Let's pray:

> *Heavenly Father, help us by Your grace and passion to value and prioritize the secret place. Holy Spirit, make the secret place a lush garden of endless delight. Turn our common places into sacred spaces. Let our bathroom floors become seas of glass; let our prayer closets become Your holy chambers; let the vehicles that we drive become fiery chariots of Your presence. Cause us to become lovers of the stillness of Your presence. Entice us by Your Spirit to dwell in the secret place, where it is simply You and me. Help us find refuge under the shelter of Your glory. Enliven us in secret and cause us to glow, radiating Your love, joy, and peace. Give us eyes that gaze for You. As we do, let us burn in union with You. Help us jealously cultivate the secret place and make us Your holy habitation. In Jesus' name I pray, amen.*

POINTS TO PONDER

- The Holy Spirit waits for me in the secret place.

- I must set aside intentional time to be in the secret place.

- The spaces I frequent daily—my living room, bedroom, or closet—can become places to be with God in secret.

- I receive of the Holy Spirit when I dwell in the shelter of God's presence.

Chapter 2

THE SECOND SECRET: BECOMING SPIRITUAL FIRST

I REMEMBER WHEN MY wife, Zuly, gave birth to our daughter, Zoey. There were so many complications with my wife's pregnancy that she needed an emergency C-section. Every time Zuly had a contraction, the baby's heart would stop beating. It was terrifying! We were rushed into the operating room, and I held my trembling wife's hand as the doctors performed the C-section.

So many thoughts rushed through my mind. I was nervous and terrified, but I kept my composure, hoping to give Zuly strength and comfort. Then suddenly in the middle of the ordeal, I heard the baby screaming. Without thinking, I jumped up to see her, and the doctor escorted me to where she was being cleaned up. As I looked at her screaming face, tears streamed down my cheeks. My heart was filled with such peace and joy.

I can't count the times over the previous nine months I put my hand on Zuly's womb and sang over Zoey, or got my guitar and sang worship songs to her, or talked to her about my day as if she could hear me in the womb. Thinking about all the times I sang and called Zoey's name, I called out to her as she was screaming in the doctor's arms. The minute I said, "Zoey," she instantly stopped crying and looked directly at me.

That's when the tears really began to flow. She recognized my voice! When the doctor handed her to me, I just stared at her. Our bond was immediate. Zoey was born for love, intimacy, connection, and purpose—like all of us. She recognized me the day she was born, even though she hadn't been able to see me for the nine months she was growing in Zuly's womb. She was developing her little senses, and in time she would grow into the vibrant little girl she is today.

When babies come into this world, they don't need to do or acquire anything more to become amazing. Give them love, care, and nurturing, and they will grow. They don't have to be taught to see, touch, or feel. Those senses are already hardwired into their tiny bodies and naturally develop with time, connection, and care from their parents.

Just as a baby is born into this world with a body that simply needs to develop and grow, so it is with us. When we are born again, we receive a regenerated, recreated spirit. What we need to grow in the spirit is already part of us. However, as newborn babies must learn to live in this natural world, so too we must learn to live and move in the realm of the spirit. This is how we lead a spiritually extraordinary life.

Your spirit is the reborn part of you, the part that connects with God's Spirit, creating a unique and profound bond. The Bible tells us, "He who is joined to the Lord is one spirit with Him" (1 Cor. 6:17). We are united with God in spirit. Your spirit is like the hidden person within your innermost core. It's the vessel of God's very breath within us. As Proverbs 20:27 puts it, "The spirit of a man is the lamp of the LORD, searching all the inner depths of his heart."

Here's a mind-blowing thought: "'Eye has not seen, nor ear heard, nor have entered into the heart of man the things which God has prepared for those who love Him.' But God has revealed them to us through His Spirit. For the Spirit searches all things, yes, the deep things of God" (1 Cor. 2:9–10). God spills His secrets through His Spirit, who searches the deep things of God.

Your spirit is this incredible link between your soul and body. It has a profound impact on both. Just as God is mysteriously one yet three, so is man: spirit, soul, and body. Just as wind cannot be seen but is experienced, so it is with the spirit of man. It can sense and perceive the spirit realm. But to get to that place in your relationship with God and become strong spiritually, you must put the Spirit first.

Just as God is Spirit, so is man because we are made in His image (Gen. 1:26). In the words of Job 32:8, "there is a spirit in man, and the breath of the Almighty gives him understanding." Understanding is not just your thoughts; it comes from the Spirit of God to your spirit.

Wrapping up his letter to the Thessalonian church, Paul leaves us with a beautiful blessing that unveils our connection with God.

> Now may the God of peace Himself sanctify you completely; and may your whole spirit, soul, and body be preserved blameless at the coming of our Lord Jesus Christ. He who calls you is faithful, who also will do it.
> —1 THESSALONIANS 5:23-24

Notice he says, "may the God of peace Himself sanctify you completely." There is a wholeness or completeness in the born-again child of God. The Greek word translated "body" in this passage is *sōma*. It refers to the "body (as a sound whole)."[1] I want you to see the mind of God in this verse. Let's look at it again: "May the God of peace Himself sanctify you completely; and may your whole spirit, soul, and body be preserved" (1 Thess. 5:23). Notice that neither body nor soul are mentioned first; spirit is. This is not by chance; the order matters.

We are spirit, soul, and body, and we must walk and move in the spirit. Take a moment to appreciate the wisdom of God here. Notice how your spirit takes the spotlight first. True people of God make it a priority to honor their spirit, allowing it to lead the way in their daily lives. It's about putting your spirit at the forefront of everything. We must become *spiritual first*.

BODY, SOUL, AND SPIRIT

Again, Proverbs 20:27 says, "The spirit of a man is the lamp of the LORD, searching all the inner depths of his heart." Here the human spirit is likened to a lamp, but not just any lamp; it is God's lamp that searches the inner depths of the heart.

Jesus gives us another perspective on the human spirit in John 7:37–39:

> On the last day, that great day of the feast, Jesus stood and cried out, saying, "If anyone thirsts, let him come to Me and drink. He who believes in Me, as the Scripture has said, out of his heart will flow rivers of living water." But this He spoke concerning the Spirit, whom those believing in Him would receive.

Now then, where is your spirit? The answer is twofold. John 7 tells us that the Spirit of God resides in you—within your innermost being. The Greek word translated "heart" in John 7:37 is *koilia*. It speaks of the belly or abdomen in general terms, covering any organ in the area of the stomach or womb. It refers to "the place where the [fetus] is conceived and nourished till birth."[2] This image is staggeringly beautiful. Where God resides within us is the place of birth. He is not in your body or soul but in the innermost part of you.

Ecclesiastes gives us further insight into the difference between the spirit and body.

> Who knows the *spirit* of the sons of men, which goes upward.
> —ECCLESIASTES 3:21, EMPHASIS ADDED

> Then the dust [our physical bodies] will return to the earth as it was, and the spirit will return to God who gave it.
> —ECCLESIASTES 12:7

These verses make it clear that the body and spirit are two separate things. The body goes to the dust; the spirit returns to God, who gave it. This is illustrated in Acts 7, where we read about the stoning of Stephen. Near the end of his life when he's being stoned and is about to be received in glory, Stephen says, "Lord Jesus, receive my *spirit*" (Acts 7:59, emphasis added). Stephen's spirit came from God and upon his death returned to Him.

There are two primary terms in Scripture translated "spirit." The first is the Hebrew word *rûaḥ* (or *ruach*), which is translated "breath," "wind," and "mind."[3] The second is the Greek word *pneuma*, which can also mean "breath."[4] Wind or breath is what distinguishes a living being from a dead body.

In Hebrew three words are used for the soul: *nep̄eš*, *rûaḥ*, and *nešāmâ*. The first and second are the most important, indicating respectively the personal soul and the invading spirit. *Nep̄eš* (or *nefesh*), translated "breath," refers predominantly to the emotional life.[5] And in addition to being translated "wind," *rûaḥ* speaks of the supernatural influence acting on man from without.[6]

Interestingly, *nešāmâ* (or *neshama*) has a dual meaning, referring both to the wind and bidding of God and the inner life in general, the emotional part of you. We understand that emotional part to be the soul.[7]

OUR BORN-AGAIN NATURE

As previously mentioned, God is connected to your spirit, the inner part of you. That is your born-again nature foretold in Ezekiel 36:26–27:

> I will give you a new heart and put a new spirit within you; I will take the heart of stone out

of your flesh and give you a heart of flesh. I
will put My Spirit within you and cause you
to walk in My statutes, and you will keep My
judgments and do them.

Here Ezekiel is prophesying about the new birth
to be given not just to the people of Israel but eventually to everyone who receives the Messiah. God
describes a sprinkling of clean water, a removal of
filthiness and idols, and says He will remove "the
heart of stone out of your flesh" (Ezek. 36:26). That's
your old life being replaced with a new, sensitive
heart—your born-again nature. Then He says, "I
will put My Spirit within you" (v. 27). Again, where
does He place the Spirit? Within *your* spirit.

So your spirit is your born-again nature. With
that in view, consider Paul's words to the Ephesians:

And you He made alive, who were dead in
trespasses and sins, in which you once walked
according to the course of this world....But
God, who is rich in mercy, because of His
great love with which He loved us, even when
we were dead in trespasses, made us alive
together with Christ (by grace you have been
saved), and raised us up together, and made us
sit together in the heavenly places in Christ
Jesus, that in the ages to come He might show
the exceeding riches of His grace in His kind-
ness toward us in Christ Jesus. For by grace

you have been saved through faith, and that
not of yourselves; it is the gift of God, not of
works, lest anyone should boast.

—EPHESIANS 2:1–2, 4–9

How does this relate to our spirits? Before Jesus
came into our lives, we were dead in our trespasses
and sins. If you are now in Christ, He has made you
alive by His Spirit *in your spirit*. The child of God
has been born again from above. Your spirit has
been born again to perceive and know God. He has
made you alive by the work of the gospel, and the
Spirit of God in your spirit enlivens you to know Him.

Jesus did not come to make bad people good; He
came to bring dead people to life. Jesus is the resurrection. Those who receive Jesus are now enlivened
and share in His resurrection power.

NEW LIFE

If you've received Jesus, you now have the newness
of life. Paul wrote in Ephesians 4:17–20:

> This I say, therefore, and testify in the Lord,
> that you should no longer walk as the rest of
> the Gentiles walk, in the futility of their mind,
> having their understanding darkened, being
> alienated from the life of God, because of the
> ignorance that is in them, because of the blind-
> ness of their heart; who, being past feeling,
> have given themselves over to lewdness, to

work all uncleanness with greediness. But you
have not so learned Christ.

Remember what Job said—that "the breath of the
Almighty gives [the spirit of man] understanding"
(Job 32:8)? Paul tells us in Ephesians 4 to not walk as
the rest of the Gentiles walk, in the futility of their
minds. To do so is both futile and vain. Without
Jesus the spirit of man is darkened. It is dead. Why?
Because it is alienated from the life of God, who is
the Spirit.

THE CHILD OF GOD HAS BEEN
BORN AGAIN FROM ABOVE.

The life of God is the Spirit of God. How do we
know this? Romans 8:2 tells us, "For the law of the
Spirit of life in Christ Jesus has made me free from
the law of sin and death." Those who do not know
Jesus as their Messiah have their minds darkened.
They are separated from the life of God because of
the blindness of their hearts.

You see, this is a spiritual thing. Again, Paul says,
"Being past feeling, [the carnal Gentiles] have given
themselves over to lewdness, to work all uncleanness with greediness" (Eph. 4:19). Do you see this?
The spirit of man is the part that is connected to
God. If you're a child of God, your spirit is connected to God. If you're not a child of God, the

reality is that your spirit is alienated, "past feeling," and not comprehending the things of God.

"But you have not so learned Christ," Paul writes, "if indeed you have heard Him and have been taught by Him, as the truth is in Jesus: that you put off, concerning your former conduct, the old man which grows corrupt according to the deceitful lusts, and be renewed in the spirit of your mind, and that you put on the new man which was created according to God, in true righteousness and holiness" (Eph. 4:20–24).

The old man was our dark and alienated spirit that had been severed from the life of God. We were dead in our sin. But now we are new creations. The new man is not the exterior; it's the interior. It is the inward spirit—the soul of man. Paul is saying to put off your former conduct, which was driven by your old lusts and desires rather than the Spirit of God and the new nature He infused into you.

John 1 tells us Jesus "was the true Light which gives light to every man coming into the world.... As many as received Him, to them He gave the right to become children of God, to those who believe in His name" (vv. 9, 12). We are born again by the Spirit of God. As we have already seen, God is searching for those who would "worship Him...in spirit and truth" (John 4:24). The way we come to Him is by receiving Jesus and having our spirits enlivened so we can approach Him.

BORN AGAIN THROUGH
THE HOLY SPIRIT

First Peter 1:23 tells us we have "been born again, not of corruptible seed but incorruptible, through the [Word] of God which lives and abides forever." Our dead spirit has become enlivened by the Word of God. The Greek term referring to the Word of God in this verse is *Logos*, the same word used in John 1:14 that states that Jesus is the Word who became flesh and dwelled among us.[8] This "word" is not the Greek *graphē* which means "scripture."[9] It is Jesus Himself, the One of whom the Scriptures testify. We see this distinction when Jesus rebuked the Pharisees, saying, "You search the Scriptures, for in them you think you have eternal life; and these are they which testify of Me. But you are not willing to come to Me that you may have life" (John 5:39–40). The Scriptures always point to the Word of God, who is Jesus.

There are three who bear witness—the Father, the Word, and the Spirit—and they all agree. How do we know this? Because we read in John 1:1–2 that "in the beginning was the Word, and the Word was with God, and the Word was God. He was in the beginning with God."

We are now the children of God because we have been born again and have received the Spirit of God. Hebrews 12:9 declares, "Furthermore, we have had human fathers who corrected us, and we paid them respect. Shall we not much more readily be in subjection to the Father of spirits and live?" You see, God has become our Father by the Spirit.

UNION WITH GOD'S SPIRIT

To the church of Corinth, Paul wrote:

> Do you not know that your bodies are members of Christ? Shall I then take the members of Christ and make them members of a harlot? Certainly not! Or do you not know that he who is joined to a harlot is one body with her? For "the two," He says, "shall become one flesh." But he who is joined to the Lord is one spirit with Him.
>
> —1 CORINTHIANS 6:15–17

He's rebuking them because of their sexual immorality, but he makes a larger point using marriage as an illustration. In marriage, which is the most intimate human relationship, the husband and wife become one flesh through their sexual union. But there is a deeper union still, one that bypasses even the intimacy of two bodies becoming one—God's Spirit and your spirit being joined. You become not one in the flesh but one in the Spirit. Remember, Jesus told us the spirit is in the innermost part, in the place of the womb.

So we see there is a union for those who have

received Jesus. Again, Jesus said, "He who believes in Me, as the Scripture has said, out of his [innermost being] will flow rivers of living water" (John 7:38). The rivers of living water are God's Spirit. And the rivers of living water reside in the innermost being.

LIVING ACCORDING TO THE SPIRIT

Let's return to 1 Thessalonians 5:23–24 (emphasis added):

> Now may the God of peace Himself sanctify you completely; and may your whole *spirit, soul, and body* be preserved blameless at the coming of our Lord Jesus Christ. He who calls you is faithful, who also will do it.

Again, through the Spirit-breathed penmanship of the apostle Paul, there is a principle for us to contemplate: that we must become spiritually minded. We must become aware of and prioritize our spirits, or our spiritual well-being, above our souls and even our bodies. Yes, we need to take care of our bodies. And yes, we need to be sound in our souls. But we must first give attention to the spirit so the soul and body can align with it.

How do we become spiritually minded? First, look to the order Paul gave in 1 Thessalonians 5:23: spirit, soul, and then body. We must ask the Holy Spirit to help us become spirit-first, spirit-dominant people who prioritize the spiritual being above all else. Many people prioritize their physical health or advancing their careers. But as people of God, we must prioritize the spirit.

Paul says in Romans 8:5, "For those who live according to the flesh set their minds on the things of the flesh [humanity's fallen nature], but those who live according to the Spirit, the things of the Spirit." Another way of saying this is those who live according to the Spirit *set their minds* on the things of the Spirit.

The flesh has its own set of impulses, desires, and perceptions. The more you let these impulses rule your life, the more entangled you get in worldly pursuits. It's a path that leads to death and separation from the things of God. But here's the good news: Your spirit comes with its own set of impulses, desires, and perceptions that are all about engaging with God. When you start tuning in to these spiritual cues, you're in for a life filled with God's life and peace. Now, don't get too comfy, because as long as you're in this world, there's going to be a bit of a tussle between your flesh and spirit. It's just part of the deal—the ongoing battle within us between the earthly, or carnal, and the spiritual.

Paul goes on to say, "For to be carnally minded is death" (Rom. 8:6). Living according to the dictates of one's carnal thinking leads to death and alienation from the things of the Spirit of God. "But to be spiritually minded is life and peace" (Rom. 8:6). So again, how do we become spiritually minded? By setting our minds on the Spirit, by giving place and attention to the Spirit, and by becoming aware of our spiritual life. "The carnal mind is enmity against God" (Rom. 8:7). In other words, carnal thinking is always obstinate. It hates and resists the things of God.

For the carnal mind "is not subject to the law of God, nor indeed can be. So then, those who are in the flesh cannot please God. But you are not in the flesh but in the Spirit" (Rom. 8:7–9). Why? Because you've received the Spirit. "You are...in the Spirit, if indeed the Spirit of God dwells in you. Now if anyone does not have the Spirit of Christ, he is not His. And if Christ is in you, the body is dead because of sin, but the Spirit is life because of righteousness" (Rom. 8:9–10). In other words, your spirit is now alive because of what Christ has done.

PRIORITIZING THE SPIRIT

And if the Spirit of Him Who raised up Jesus from the dead dwells in you, [then] He Who raised up Christ Jesus from the dead will also restore to life your mortal (short-lived, perishable) bodies through His Spirit Who dwells in you.

—ROMANS 8:11, AMPC

Paul is speaking of our lives right now. He who raised Christ from the dead will also give life to "your mortal (short-lived, perishable) bodies." How? Through the Spirit who dwells in you. Yet people often fail to prioritize their spirits.

Many people make space for their finances, and there's nothing wrong with that. Many people make space for their plans or space to take care of their appearance. Again, there's nothing wrong with these things in and of themselves. But we must be a people who take care of our spirits and our spiritual well-being. Your soul—your mind, will, and emotions—is in a constant dance between your spirit and your flesh. What captures your mind is what gains a foothold.

Now, how do we make space for our spirits? It's simple—by making room for the Word. Just as our physical bodies crave sustenance, so do our spirits. What food and water are to our bodies, the Word and the Spirit of God are to our spirits. It's as Peter says: "As newborn babes, desire the pure milk of the word, that you may grow thereby" (1 Pet. 2:2). Remember this nugget from Jesus: "It is the Spirit who gives life; the flesh profits nothing. The words that I speak to you are spirit, and they are life" (John 6:63). God's Word is like a spiritual feast providing nourishment for your innermost being.

In Proverbs 4, Solomon says, "My son, give attention to my words; incline your ear to my sayings"

(v. 20). Can you hear the heart of God in that verse? You're His child. "Do not let them depart from your eyes; keep them in the midst of your heart" (Prov. 4:21). That's being spiritually minded. "For they are life to those who find them, and health to all their flesh" (Prov. 4:22). The Word of God is like medicine.

"Keep your heart with all diligence, for out of it spring the issues of life" (Prov. 4:23). Here, Solomon says to take care of your heart, or your innermost being, "with all diligence." The Amplified Bible, Classic Edition says, "Guard your heart with all vigilance" (Prov. 4:23). The word translated "guard" is the Hebrew term *nāṣar*. *Nāṣar* means to keep, observe, and watchfully guard.[10] We need to guard our hearts with all *vigilance*. However, we can't guard our hearts too carefully since all "the issues of life" flow out of it.

How do we diligently guard our hearts from anything that would taint or corrupt them? Proverbs 4:24 says, "Put away from you a deceitful mouth, and put perverse lips far from you." This is how we guard our spiritual well-being; spiritual well-being is not just how we monitor our interior lives but also what will shape our exterior lives. "For," as Jesus said, "out of the abundance of the heart the mouth speaks" (Matt. 12:34).

Proverbs 4 goes on to say, "Let your eyes look straight ahead, and your eyelids look right before you" (v. 25). That verse may seem cryptic at first, but it makes sense both poetically and spiritually. It's also a beautiful typology of the inward life of prayer. When you close your eyes and look to the Spirit of God within, that is when you see. The path then begins to come into focus.

"Ponder the path of your feet, and let all your ways be established. Do not turn to the right or the left; remove your foot from evil" (Prov. 4:26–27). You see, there are things that pollute our hearts, and God wants our vessels to be unhindered from the free flow of God's Spirit in our lives. The Spirit of God in your spirit is like a river of living water, and the issues of life that flow in it are like rocks and stones. Do not allow the issues of life to dam up—to put a wall up against—the current of the Spirit's love.

Is there bitterness and resentment in any area of your heart? Is there unforgiveness, strife, offense, or hate? Is your heart filled with pride? All these things corrupt the heart and hinder the Spirit's reflection within us. We are meant to reflect God, spirit to Spirit. But there are many things that hinder. The writer of Hebrews instructs us to look "carefully lest anyone fall short of the grace of God; lest any root of bitterness springing up cause trouble, and by this many become defiled" (12:15). Many people become defiled by bitterness, among other things, but we do not have to be numbered among those people, especially if we are to become spiritually minded.

STEPS TO BECOMING
SPIRITUALLY MINDED

What practical steps can we take to become spiritually minded?

Mind the Spirit.

First and foremost, we must mind the Spirit. Much as being told, "Mind your manners," is a way of saying, "Pay attention to the habits you have adopted," this is a call to pay attention. In other words, to mind the Spirit is to *set your heart on things above* and apply them with biblical meditation.

Here is a practical way for you to mind the Spirit, or the things of the Spirit, found in Colossians 3:1–4:

> If then you were raised with Christ, seek those things which are above, where Christ is, sitting at the right hand of God. Set your mind on things above, not on things on the earth. For you died, and your life is hidden with Christ in God. When Christ who is our life appears, then you also will appear with Him in glory.

This is not a native practice for any of us; it has to be nurtured. We must learn to set our minds on things above. Every time you focus on the Holy Spirit, you are setting your mind on things above. Anytime you read the Scriptures, you are setting your mind on things above. Anytime you contemplate the gospel, you are setting your mind on things above. Every time you pray, you are setting your mind on things above.

Doing this will reveal other changes you may need to make. What is robbing you of joy? Identify those things and remove them from your life. This is also a step in minding the Spirit. Maybe what God reveals is not outright sin but just something that is fleshly. According to 1 Corinthians 3, carnality can manifest in different ways—as division, strife, factions, assuming your way of thinking is the best way, and preferring to see certain people in church rather than seeing every believer as God's child. To combat this, you must acknowledge the Lord continually throughout your day. As Psalm 16:8 says, you must "set the LORD always before [you]."

Learn to acknowledge the Lord continually.

Many people limit God to just their prayer times, not realizing that we are called to acknowledge Him continually throughout our days. Jesus said He is the true Shepherd, and those who come to Him must go in and out of Him and find pasture (John 10:9–11). There are times when we go into the presence of the Lord and feast from the hand of our Shepherd, and there are times when we come out of our prayer and continually meet the Good Shepherd. Learn to acknowledge the Lord throughout your whole day. He is ever with us, both in our moments of solitude and our moments with others through the hustle and bustle of the day.

Live a life of prayer.

Prayer isn't limited to getting on your knees for an hour. That's good, and you should do that. But prayer is chiefly the acknowledgment of the presence of the Lord in your life. Prayer is becoming aware of God. It is a way of receiving His loving gaze upon us and meeting His loving gaze. In the words of A. W. Tozer, "When the eyes of the soul looking out meet the eyes of God looking in, heaven has begun right here on this earth."[11]

Live a life of worship and praise.

The language of the Spirit is a language of praise. In John 4:23 Jesus says that God is looking for those who would worship Him in spirit and truth (NLT). You want to strengthen your spirit? You want to mind the Spirit? You want to live Spirit first? Live a life of praise and worship!

Get rid of distractions.

Abstain for a time from things that deter you from minding your spirit and instead focus on the Lord. Now, please understand that we are saved by the pure grace and mercy of God. I am not suggesting that you work for your salvation but that you walk from the gift of salvation inside you. Things such as distractions, cares, and bitterness poison the wells of our hearts and cause us to walk about frustrated, confused, and upset. Let that not be said of you!

BENEFITS OF BEING SPIRITUALLY MINDED

What are the benefits of being spiritually minded?

Life and peace

In the Book of Romans, Paul says that "to be spiritually minded is life and peace" (8:6). So life and peace are the first benefits of being spiritually minded. When you are spiritually minded, you will know life in the Spirit and a peace that is uncontainable. And when the issues and the trials of life come, you will be as cool, levelheaded, and calm as you've ever been. You will have a peace that is not yours but His.

Renewed joy in our salvation

Another benefit of being spiritually minded is that you remember the joy of your salvation. Psalm 103:2 tells us to "forget not all His benefits," but we so easily do! We forget the Lord when we aren't spiritually sensitive and devoted to Him. When we "forget not all His benefits," the joy of our salvation will be restored.

Desire for the Word

Another benefit of becoming spiritually aware is that you will gain a fresh desire for the Word of God.

43

All of a sudden you will "desire the pure milk of the word, that you may grow thereby" (1 Pet. 2:2). Here is a powerful truth: You are born again through the Word of God, and as a child of God, you are nourished through the Word. You are fed and you grow by learning and applying the Scriptures. As you learn to mind the Spirit and set your attention on things above, you gain a fresh desire for the Word and for prayer, and a deep yearning to know the Lord more.

A hatred for sin

When we have a relationship with the Lord, we also develop a new relationship with sin. Do we still sin? Yes. Do we sin daily? Yes! But there is a difference between leading a life of sin and walking after the Spirit in the midst of our sinful lives. When you are spiritually minded, you will hate sin.

The fruit of the Spirit

Finally, being spiritually minded causes us to cultivate the fruit of the Holy Spirit. Do you want the love of God to be evident in your life? Do you want unshakable peace no matter what comes your way? Do you want self-control over the appetites of the flesh? Then become spiritually minded. Guard your heart and develop a lifestyle of drawing near to God. When you do these things, the effects of the Holy Spirit become evident.

LIVING IN VICTORY

This is the fruit of walking in the Spirit: You'll have a love that is His, a joy that is His, and self-control that is His. Maybe you are trying hard in your own strength to overcome sin. The reality is that if you minister to the Spirit and surrender yourself to the grace of God, you will walk in the fruit of the Spirit. You will have a desire for more and more of the Spirit and to live a life that is pleasing to the Lord. And you will have a disdain and distaste for the things of the flesh.

So again, if you want to be spiritually minded and put your spirit first, eliminate distractions. Surrender yourself to God in prayer. Offer your time to Him. Share your need with Him. Ask the Holy Spirit to help you acknowledge His presence throughout your day. Learn to guard your heart and avoid things that contaminate your spiritual well-being. Maybe it's gossip; maybe it's slander; maybe you're giving yourself over to certain vices; maybe your mindset is not pleasing to the Lord, or you're struggling with feelings of inferiority, guilt, and shame. Whatever it is, give that over to the Lord to become spiritually minded in *all* things.

Just as the benefits of being spiritually minded show, so do the effects of not putting our spirits first. When we are not spiritually minded, our desires are contrary to the Word, we want to do things that gratify only our flesh, and our desire for God begins to wane.

If you're finding yourself in that predicament, throw yourself into the presence of the Lord. If you've repented of your sin and confessed Jesus as your Lord and Savior, you're a child of God and you belong to Him. Align your thinking to agree with how God truly sees you, and believe He desires to be close to you. Some of your problems may be because you don't believe God wants you close to Him. Satan is a liar! The Bible says the Spirit of God yearns jealously for you. (See 2 Corinthians 11:2.) He wants you more than you want Him—so much so that He sent His Son to die for you.

The Lord wants you to become spiritually minded. He wants the Spirit of God inside your spirit to dominate your flesh, give you a new outlook, and cause you to walk in victory.

SURRENDER AND REST

We often struggle and strive and sometimes do not feel worthy of God's care, unconditional love, and unmerited grace. If we are honest, we sometimes fail to realize how good God truly is, and we need to remind ourselves that all those thoughts and emotions are not the lens through which our Father sees us. We are so used to thoughts of negativity fueled by our performances, or the lack thereof, that we tend to feel God is distant from us and we somehow do not measure up to Him. We have the mindset of an old wineskin and wonder why we cannot drink the new wine.

We have to change our thinking and shed these distractions. By allowing God's grace, through His Word and Spirit, to shape us into new wineskins, we can receive the eternal water of His presence. Just as my love for my daughter was instant when she was born into this world because she came from me, the Father's love for you is instant. He wants to so fill your life that His presence permeates your being. This is what the spiritual walk looks like.

Surrender and rest accelerate us into the flow of prayer. Anytime mindsets and attitudes rise in your soul that are contrary to the work of the gospel, surrender into God's presence and rest. Those who depend on the Spirit, who lean upon the Word of God, and who bask in His love are propelled forward in their walk with God. That's what grace looks like in movement.

Do not allow your cares, condemnation, bouts of frustration, and distractions keep you from intimacy with the Holy Spirit. The secret place is the womb of spiritual nourishment and wholeness. When you find yourself kicking and screaming because of life's trials, rest in His ever-present presence. Surrender into Him. He's with you—closer than your breath, deeper than your thoughts, and more faithful than your feelings. You were born for intimacy!

Let's pray:

> Heavenly Father, show me by Your grace and unlimited love that I have been born from above. I was born to be intimate with You. Holy Spirit, reveal the companionship and communion that have already been hard-wired into my spirit. Reveal to me that all things as it relates to life and godliness have already been granted to me by Your Spirit and Word. Remove old wineskins—old patterns of thinking that are not in alignment with my new nature in You.
>
> Grant me the revelation, according to Your Word and by Your Holy Spirit, that I am indeed loved and created for intimacy with You. I thank You that I have been born anew and that You are closer to me than the air that I breathe. Cause me to surrender to Your presence, and reveal to me the joy of prayer. I ask You to revive my heart, give me fresh intimacy with You, and bring me to glories I have yet to experience. In Jesus' name I pray, amen.

POINTS TO PONDER

- I am spirit, soul, and body.

- My spirit is the receiver of God's Spirit.

- I must live from the place of my spirit, not my flesh.

- I must grow by feeding my spirit the Word and by fellowshipping with the Holy Spirit.

Chapter 3

THE THIRD SECRET: MEDITATING ON GOD'S WORD

EARLY IN MY walk with Christ I went into a season of intensely studying Scripture. At times I would spend hours reading Scripture and analyzing footnotes, commentaries, and all sorts of information to help me understand the Word on an intellectual level. But something always seemed to be missing, and I could not put my finger on it.

I had read through the entire Bible and knew a lot about Scripture, and I began to grow puffed up with knowledge. I began to see others as less than because they did not know as much as I did. The Bible says, "Knowledge puffs up, but love edifies" (1 Cor. 8:1). That was the predicament I was in during that stage of my life.

I remember the first time the Holy Spirit graciously and lovingly guided me toward meditating on His Word. I was in Bible school, and on this particular weekend, I felt a deep knowing that I was to spend approximately three days in 1 John chapter 4. I just knew in my spirit that I was supposed to stay there, chew on the scripture, and expect the Holy Spirit to speak to me through the passage.

On the third day of meditating on 1 John chapter 4, the Holy Spirit highlighted a verse to me. It reads as follows:

> Beloved, let us love one another, for love is of God; and everyone who loves is born of God and knows God. He who does not love does not know God, for God is love. In this the love of God was manifested toward us, that God has sent His only begotten Son into the world, that we might live through Him.
>
> —1 JOHN 4:7–9

I must have read that verse dozens and dozens of times, but what happened that day was something I never experienced before. It was as though the very verses became a window to see the Lord in a deep and living way. It was as if the passage leaped from the Bible into my heart and became spiritual food for me. It felt as though God Himself was speaking to me and giving me revelation about how to apply His Word in my everyday life. The experience was beyond mere intellectual assent; it was revelation knowledge that went from my head to my heart. It was almost as if I could have written entire volumes of books from that single passage of Scripture. The Holy Spirit made the Bible come to life. That day, God's Word became spiritual meat.

This experience quickly drove me to my knees in absolute repentance because it was then that I realized I knew nothing. I filled my head with wonderful knowledge, but it never reached my heart and became real to me until that moment. I began to see the Scriptures not merely as a book to study but as food for the spirit. A deep value for the meat of God's Word germinated in my heart, and I developed a greater desire to know more about the revelations of the Word of God. And it all happened through meditation on the Word of God.

That is the next secret to intimacy with the Holy Spirit—to meditate on God's Word. But to truly understand how this will help us, we first must realize how priceless Scripture is. If we do not value the Word of God, we will never place our thoughts and our wills in alignment with it.

The importance of the Word is evident from the very beginning of Scripture. Genesis 1:2–3 (AMPC) declares:

> The earth was without form and an empty waste, and darkness was upon the face of the very great deep. The Spirit of God was moving (hovering, brooding) over the face of

the waters. And God said, Let there be light;
and there was light.

In this passage we see that God fashions everything by His word. It also reveals a relationship. The
Spirit of God was present with the Word of God at
the beginning, and the Word formed and fashioned
all things.

Hebrews 11:3 (AMPC) points to the same truth:

> By faith we understand that the worlds [during
> the successive ages] were framed (fashioned,
> put in order, and equipped for their intended
> purpose) by the word of God, so that what
> we see was not made out of things which are
> visible.

This parallels not only what we read in Genesis
but also John's words in his Gospel:

> In the beginning [before all time] was the
> Word (Christ), and the Word was with God,
> and the Word was God Himself. He was
> present originally with God. All things were
> made and came into existence through Him;
> and without Him was not even one thing
> made that has come into being.
>
> —JOHN 1:1–3, AMPC

The apostle Paul also echoes these themes in his
letter to the Colossians:

For it was in Him that all things were created, in heaven and on earth, things seen and things unseen, whether thrones, dominions, rulers, or authorities; all things were created and exist through Him [by His service, intervention] and in and for Him. And He Himself existed before all things, and in Him all things consist (cohere, are held together).

—COLOSSIANS 1:16–17, AMPC

Again, we see that Jesus is the Word made flesh who existed before all things, created all things, and sustains all things. The One who holds all things together is the Word of God Himself—thus, we must value the Word above all things!

THE WORD BRINGS LIGHT

Psalm 119:130–131 says, "The entrance of Your words gives light; it gives understanding to the simple. I opened my mouth and panted, for I longed for Your commandments." Where does the psalmist get this idea? He gets it from Genesis, where we read that God spoke and there was light. All things are made visible—all things are made known—by God's Word. The Word brings light, and God's desire is that you will be filled with His light—that you will be filled with His Word.

Ephesians 1:15–18 (emphasis added) says:

> Therefore I also, after I heard of your faith in
> the Lord Jesus and your love for all the saints,
> do not cease to give thanks for you, making
> mention of you in my prayers: that the God of
> our Lord Jesus Christ, the Father of glory, may
> give to you the spirit of wisdom and revela-
> tion *in the knowledge of Him*, the eyes of your
> understanding being enlightened [or, the eyes
> of your heart being flooded with light]; that
> you may know what is the hope of His calling,
> what are the riches of the glory of His inheri-
> tance in the saints.

Do you want to know the hope of your calling? Do you want to understand the great hope you've been called to? It comes only by having the eyes of your understanding, or the eyes of your heart, flooded with light. And the only way for your under- standing to be flooded with light is for you to be filled with God's Word, because the entrance of the Word brings light (Ps. 119:130).

How does that flooding of light come? First and foremost, you must be a believer in the Lord Jesus. If you read the Scriptures, you'll see that they tes- tify of the Lord, who is Himself the light. We see over and over again that God's Word brings light. If you want to be flooded with light and know the glo- rious hope of your calling in the Lord, in the full- ness of His calling, you must relish God's Word.

We read in Psalm 119:105, "Your word is a lamp

to my feet and a light to my path." That means the only way we can rightly see in life is through the light of God's Word. As we walk in the Word, we walk in the light. Not only does Jesus, the Word, light our feet, showing us where to go, but He also lights the path. He says in John 8:12, "I am the light of the world. He who follows Me shall not walk in darkness, but have the light of life." So as we walk in His Word, we walk on the right path.

Finally, I want to point out Proverbs 6:23 (AMPC): "For the commandment is a lamp, and the whole teaching [of the law] is light, and reproofs of discipline are the way of life." Again, this reminds us that God's Word must be valued. We must see His Word as light, keeping ever before us that Jesus Himself is the Word made flesh.

THE WORD NOURISHES

In the plant kingdom the trees, herbs, grass, and so on grow through photosynthesis, the process by which plants receive nutrients from light. This translates to our spiritual lives. We must receive and walk in the light of God's Word in order to be nourished.

In Matthew 4, Jesus was led by the Spirit into the wilderness to be tempted by the devil. After He fasted for forty days and forty nights, He was hungry. His physical desire was to eat, and the enemy seized this opportunity to tempt Him.

> Now when the tempter came to Him, he said, "If You are the Son of God, command that these stones become bread." But He answered and said, "It is written, 'Man shall not live by bread alone, but by every word that proceeds from the mouth of God.'"
>
> —MATTHEW 4:3–4

Jesus tells us that just as our bodies need bread to live, so our spirits need every word that comes out of the mouth of God to sustain us.

In the Book of Isaiah there's an interesting parallel between nourishment and the Word:

> For as the rain comes down, and the snow from heaven, and do not return there, but water the earth, and make it bring forth and bud, that it may give seed to the sower and bread to the eater, so shall My word be that goes forth from My mouth; it shall not return to Me void, but it shall accomplish what I please, and it shall prosper in the thing for which I sent it.
>
> —ISAIAH 55:10–11

So we see that God compares His Word with rain. What does rain do? It waters crops, but its purpose doesn't stop there. Rain causes life to spring forth and bud that it may give seed to those who sow and bread to those who eat. God says, "So shall My word that goes forth from my mouth." Just as rain produces vegetation that the harvester can use to make food to consume, so God's Word brings life and nourishment to fulfill the purposes of God.

In John 6:35 Jesus says, "I am the bread of life. He who comes to Me shall never hunger, and he who believes in Me shall never thirst." Hunger and thirst are a language we all understand because all bodies need food and water to survive. This verse tells us that Jesus Himself, the Word made flesh, is the nourishment our spirits need.

These, then, are the two primary ways we understand the absolute necessity of Scripture in our lives: the Word is light, illuminating our path, and the Word is spiritual food that nourishes us.

In 1 Peter 2:1-3 the aging apostle says, "Therefore, laying aside all malice, all deceit, hypocrisy, envy, and all evil speaking, as newborn babes, desire the pure milk of the word, that you may grow thereby, if indeed you have tasted that the Lord is gracious." He is indeed a God whose goodness is meant to be tasted and who feeds His children with the spiritual milk of the Word!

God values His Word. The worlds were formed through His Word. In the Word there is life and light and nourishment. If we do not value the Word, we will never meditate on it. And if we do not meditate on the Word, we will never realize all the blessings it holds.

How do you meditate on the Word? Ask the Holy

Spirit to make the Word alive to you. Read scriptures over and over that speak of the importance of Scripture. Allow those scriptures to transform your perspective so you see the Bible not just as words on a page but as spiritual food necessary for your very survival. Many times we make the mistake of looking at the Bible as just a book we read instead of a book we need!

The Bible says, "The spirit of [man] is the lamp of the LORD, searching all the innermost parts of his being" (Prov. 20:27, NASB) and that the "word is a lamp to [our] feet" (Ps. 119:105). For us to be the light we are called to be in the world, the light of God's Word must shine brightly even in our hidden places. But it all starts with valuing the Word as the food for the spirit that it is.

When you eat in the natural, you move in the energy provided by that food. If you eat only junk food, you're going to feel like garbage. If you eat only things that are artificial, you will end up feeling sick and tired because you're consuming empty calories. In the same way, we must feed on that which is alive spiritually. Many times we feed on things that instantly gratify our cravings, but they are quick fixes that don't truly satisfy.

Spiritual nourishment is a lot like natural nourishment. Eating foods that are man-made, synthetic, and artificial harms our bodies. In a similar way, many people consume the wrong spiritual food or not enough of the right things. They get a steady stream of celebrity preachers, but their diet lacks consistent prayer. So their emotions are up and down because they are consumed with their feelings and circumstances and are not feasting on the Scriptures, which are "alive, and active" (Heb. 4:12, MEV).

The Word of God is living, and when you consume it, you move in the grace and energy of that spiritually alive nourishment. If you feast on God's Word, you will move through your day with spiritual strength. You will begin to discern spiritual truths because you will be operating from a different fuel source. Instead of the artificial sweeteners of life or the synthetic substances of sin, you will be energized by the living Word and be full of spiritual vitality.

THE WORD CLEANSES

In John's Gospel, Jesus gives us a beautiful image of what it means to depend on the Lord and His Word.

> I am the true vine, and My Father is the vine-dresser. Every branch in Me that does not bear fruit He takes away; and every branch that bears fruit He prunes, that it may bear more fruit. You are already clean because of the word which I have spoken to you. Abide in Me, and I in you. As the branch cannot bear

fruit of itself, unless it abides in the vine, neither can you, unless you abide in Me.

—JOHN 15:1–4

The word translated "prune" in verse 2 means
"to cleanse."[1] The Word, then, is not only light and
life and spiritual nourishment but also a purifying
force. Meditating on the Word brings a washing, a
deep cleansing, and a pruning.

We see this cleansing effect in Ephesians 5:25–27:

Husbands, love your wives, just as Christ also
loved the church and gave Himself for her, that
He might sanctify and cleanse her with the
washing of water by the word, that He might
present her to Himself a glorious church, not
having spot or wrinkle or any such thing, but
that she should be holy and without blemish.

Paul tells us that the water of the Word is a
cleansing agent. It washes us and presents us to
God as a purified bride. So when we study and meditate on the Word, we are approaching words that
bring light, nourishment, and cleansing. When we
see the Word this way, we will treasure it all the
more. May the Lord give us eyes to see the importance of the Word and of meditating on it, for the
Word brings life! Early on in my marriage I learned
the value and the cleansing effects my words had
over my wife. Whenever she was discouraged or had

moments when she felt defeated or times when she felt insecure, I would speak words of confidence and I would prophesy destiny into her. I would speak into her situation and affirm who she was as a mom, as a daughter of God, and as my bride. I began to notice throughout the years how she would flourish in confidence and strength because my words had cleansing and empowering effects on her. This is exactly how the bride of Christ is. There are moments when we need the affirmations and the cleansing words of God that come from the Scriptures to revive and strengthen us for the tasks and the assignments ahead.

**IF YOU FEAST ON GOD'S WORD,
YOU WILL MOVE THROUGH YOUR
DAY WITH SPIRITUAL STRENGTH.**

Jesus said in John 6:63, "It is the Spirit Who gives life [He is the Life-giver]; the flesh conveys no benefit whatever [there is no profit in it]. The words (truths) that I have been speaking to you are spirit and life" (AMPC). We must understand that when we meditate on God's Word, we receive life in every available form—as light, nourishment, and cleansing. The Word touches every dimension of the human person.

ROOTED, STABLE, AND FRUITFUL

The Bible tells us in Psalm 1:1–2: "Blessed is the man who walks not in the counsel of the ungodly, nor stands in the path of sinners, nor sits in the seat of the scornful. But his delight is in the law of the LORD, and in His law [or word] he meditates day and night." The Hebrew word translated "meditates" is *hāḡâ*, and it means to utter, mutter, or speak.[2] That is what true meditation is: uttering, pondering, and studying the Word—not only reading the Scriptures but dwelling on them.

The psalmist tells us that those who meditate on the Word will notice its effects.

> He shall be like a tree planted by the rivers of water, that brings forth its fruit in its season, whose leaf also shall not wither; and whatever he does shall prosper.
>
> —PSALM 1:3

Those who meditate on God's Word shall be like a tree. Trees planted beside water are firm and stable. Their roots go deep into the ground. Those who meditate on God's Word are stable; they are rooted. They are whole, and they are planted by rivers of water—not just one river, but *rivers* of water.

Rivers represent the Spirit and the Word. So those who meditate on Scripture are full of the Spirit. They are full of the life-bringing, cleansing water that nourishes and that causes the tree to bring forth its fruit in its season. Jesus said in John 15:8, "By this is my Father glorified, that you bear much fruit." Fruitfulness is a sign that we are abiding in the Word made flesh, Jesus, and in the written Word.

Notice again that Psalm 1:3 says, "He shall be like a tree planted by the rivers of water, that brings forth its fruit in its season, *whose leaf also shall not wither*" (emphasis added). I find that last phrase interesting, because as seasons change, leaves wither. But those who are fixed on the Word of God will have green leaves despite the seasons of life. Why? Because they are planted. They are fixed near the streams of life, so whatever they do or touch will prosper.

Again, we gain spiritual prosperity and vitality as we meditate on God's Word. As you reflect on the Scriptures, contemplating them and thinking them through, you will find firmness, rootedness, fruitfulness, and prosperity. And it all begins with valuing the Word—with seeing it as food for your spirit and a light for our path.

We see this also in the Book of Joshua. God told him, "This Book of the Law shall not depart from your mouth, but you shall meditate in it day and night, that you may observe to do according to all that is written in it. For then you will make your way prosperous, and then you will have good success" (Josh. 1:8). That's what God wants for you, day and night, as you fill your mind and heart with His words.

Friend, is your life spiritually unstable? Are you constantly up and down, swayed by every opinion that comes your way? If so, return to the Word of God and meditate on it day and night.

HOW TO MEDITATE ON THE WORD

You may be wondering how, practically speaking, you meditate on the Word. You can begin by silently reading the Scriptures. Put away the noise and distractions. Put away the cares, and still your mind and heart so you can focus on the Word.

My dear friend Eric Gilmour says silence is not the "absence of external noise but...the absence of internal noise."[3] Often we are busy, distracted, and flooded with so many thoughts that we can't properly meditate on God's Word. Do what helps you be still inwardly. Maybe you need to sit down, or perhaps it helps you to go for a walk. Or maybe you just need to step outside for a minute to collect yourself. For some, putting on instrumental worship helps them focus on the things of God to get to a place of inward stillness. Do whatever you need to do; then begin to read!

As you read the Word with your heart and mind still and focused, contemplate and dwell on what is being said. At this point, read the Scriptures out loud; you may even adapt what you're reading into prayers. Relish every verse. Read the Scriptures slowly and focus on every single word. Don't worry about whether you get through a whole chapter. Just get yourself to a place where you prayerfully engage with what you're reading.

Another way you can meditate on God's Word is to sing it out to God. *The aim of meditating on God's Word is not simply memorization but internalization.* The point is to get it in you. Internalize the Word by reading and chewing on it, allowing it to get deep into your heart and soul. There's nothing wrong with memorizing scriptures, but many times we stop there. We fill our minds with knowledge of the Word, but growth happens when we apply it. We have to let it go deeper and take root in our spirits. It has to go so deep that it becomes part of us.

Have you ever heard someone say, "Chew on this for a second"? Here's some food for thought: Begin to chew the Word. Read a passage and then read it again. Then read it in context. Take a verse and begin to dissect it. Chew on it by reading it over and over. This is how you internalize the Word in such a way that you gain revelation. There is no new revelation. All the revelation is in Scripture. As we prayerfully meditate on God's Word, we receive the insight and revelation found within it.

Think about the process of eating. You see the food in front of you. Then you hold it in your hand, bite it, and chew on it. You must chew it before you can swallow and digest it. When the food goes into your belly, it then becomes a part of you. When it becomes a part of you, it gives you strength and nourishment. That is what meditating on God's Word looks like. You take the Word, read it, chew on it, and then internalize it. Once you do those things, it goes into your innermost being and strengthens your spirit.

BEGIN TO CHEW THE WORD.

Internalizing the Word of God produces life, makes your life fruitful, and helps you get God's perspective—His way of looking at things. When you allow the Word to become a part of you, you become, as the apostle Paul said, a living "epistle... [being] known and read by all men (2 Cor. 3:2). You become so full of the Word and Spirit of God that you become a living epistle being read by everyone you see.

EAT AND DRINK!

Many people dream of having a perfect physique, so they do everything from hyperintense cardio workouts to starving themselves. Yet 80 percent of a complete body transformation consists of changing what you eat and drink. A staggering 80 percent of the transformation is based on your diet![4]

In the same way, the key to a spiritual metamorphosis is your spiritual diet. Yet all too often believers do not know that their spirits are starving and neglected, and many walk about with emaciated, atrophied spirits. If you want to be spiritually healthy and strong, begin to eat and drink!

In the Book of Exodus we see something quite peculiar:

> Then Moses went up, also Aaron, Nadab, and Abihu, and seventy of the elders of Israel, *and they saw the God of Israel.* And there was under His feet as it were a paved work of sapphire stone, and it was like the very heavens in its clarity. But on the nobles of the children of Israel He did not lay His hand. *So they saw God, and they ate and drank.* Then the LORD said to Moses, "Come up to Me on the mountain and be there; and I will give you tablets of stone, and the law and commandments which I have written, that you may teach them."
> —EXODUS 24:9–12, EMPHASIS ADDED

When the elders of Israel saw God, they ate and drank; this was a sign of their communion and fellowship with God. Do you want to see God? Eat and drink! God is a feast; what bread is for the body, the bread of His presence is for the Spirit, and what water is for the body, the cleansing water of the Word is to your spirit. We must eat and drink! Eating and drinking God's Word and presence are what give us spiritual vitality! Prayer is the drink; the Word is your spiritual food.

"Man does not live by bread alone, but by every word that comes from the mouth of God" (Matt. 4:4, NET). The Word must be your daily bread. Feasting on Scripture as food is the essence of meditation.

Remember Joshua 1:8: "This Book of the Law shall not depart from your mouth, but you shall meditate in it day and night." As I mentioned previously, the Hebrew word translated "meditate" is *hāĝâ*, which *Brown-Driver-Briggs Hebrew and English Lexicon* defines as "inarticulate sounds...[to] growl...groan, moan...utter...(soliloquize) meditate, muse... imagine, devise."[5] The related words *hegeh* and *higgayon* refer to "a rumbling, growling sound...a moaning...a sigh or moan" and "resounding music, meditation, [and] musing," respectively.[6]

In other words, we are to utter, moan, speak, muse, imagine, and even sing God's Word. Paul conveyed this idea in Ephesians 5:18–19:

> And do not be drunk with wine, in which is dissipation; but be filled with the Spirit, speaking to one another in psalms and hymns and spiritual songs, singing and making melody in your heart to the Lord.

God's Word must become the melody we hang our lives on, the moan of our spirits. The Word must be planted so deep within us that it is the groan of our hearts as we cry out for more of Him!

REVELATION THROUGH THE WORD

As I've said, it is not enough merely to know the Word intellectually; we must have it revealed to our spirits by God's Spirit. That only happens when the Word gets into the depths of us—when Scripture is not just read or heard but ingested and digested.

Again, the way to receive this revelation is by meditating on the Word. Revelation is an unveiling of what God has already said in the Scriptures. By His Holy Spirit, God reveals and illuminates the scriptures that you meditate on for the purpose of receiving Him the way He intended you to. "All Scripture is God-breathed" (2 Tim. 3:16, NIV), and it is opened up to us by His Spirit. The Spirit will never reveal something that contradicts God's written Word; it is the revelation of the written Word that brings life and transformation. Eating and drinking of God's Spirit and Word bring us closer to Him. This creates communion—which gives birth to revelation—for you and for the people of God writ large.

The Pharisees knew the Scriptures, but they missed the Word made flesh when He was standing right in front of them! They knew about the Law and memorized it, but when the Word was made visible, they could not see Him. They had understanding, but they did not have revelation. So I encourage you to read the Word of God prayerfully and ask the Holy Spirit to unveil the Scriptures to you. As you do that and chew on God's Word, it will go deep inside you, bringing spiritual light, nourishment, cleansing, and strength.

If you want God to speak to you, get in the Word! If you want a prophetic word, open your Bible. If you want to know what God sounds like, read the Scriptures. Value the Word and receive guidance, insight, fruitfulness, and true biblical prosperity. If you want balance and wholeness in your walk with God, meditate on His Word. If you want to stop being unstable, get in the Word. It is like a window to help you properly see through Him.

To behold the Lord in His glory is to behold His Word. The written Word, the spoken Word, and the living Word—they all speak of Jesus. If you want to know what Jesus is like, if you want to understand the wonders of His person and be captivated by His beauty, then you have to value the Word. The Lord will never separate Himself from His Word; they are truly one.

Meditating on God's Word will expose what is and is not God in your life. It will cause you to grow in discernment. God will begin to show you what are soulish, emotional responses and what is from His Spirit. Your soul (mind, will, and emotions) and spirit (the part of you connected to God) are inseparable. The only way to separate the soul from the spirit is through the Word. The Word cuts you, "piercing even to the division of soul and spirit" (Heb. 4:12). The more you seek the Lord through His Word, the more you will hear Him say by His Spirit, "This is of Me, but that is not of Me."

Many times we are conflicted in prayer. We're trying to figure out God's will for our lives or what He is saying in a particular season, and we get frustrated because we don't hear the Lord's voice. Could it be that we're not discerning the will of God because we're not getting into the Word?

I encourage you to spend time with the Spirit and in the Word. If you've never meditated on the Word, stop for five minutes at the start of your day or before you go to bed, read a few verses, and allow the Holy Spirit to speak to you. As you relish the Word, God's Spirit will breathe life into you; bring light, insight, and illumination; and fill you with the knowledge of His will.

Pray with me:

> *Heavenly Father, I come to You in the mighty name of Jesus. I agree with the power of Your Word and with its effects and cleansing properties. The entrance of Your Word brings light. Holy Spirit, grant*

me the spirit of wisdom and revelation and the deep and intimate knowledge of You by having the eyes of my heart flooded with light. Show me with revelation the knowledge that proceeds from Your Spirit. As I meditate upon the Word of God, illuminate and reveal Your voice to me. Let the verses of the Scriptures become windows through which I see You more clearly, and cause me to see Your Word as true food for my spirit and renewal for my soul. In Jesus' name I pray, amen!

POINTS TO PONDER

- Biblical meditation is internalizing the Scriptures within my heart.

- God wants to reveal to me His Word by His Spirit.

- I must nourish my spirit just as I nourish my physical body.

- I must eat and drink God's Word and presence daily to grow spiritually.

THE FOURTH SECRET: WAITING BEFORE THE LORD

ONCE HEARD A powerful minister of the gospel say the secret of his ministry was waiting before the Lord. I remember being so enthralled with the way he ministered the Spirit to others. When he moved, God moved. It was almost as if he was one with the Spirit of God. The times I had the privilege of attending his meetings, I could feel the tangible glory of the Lord on and around him.

There was a season when the Lord used him indirectly to teach me how to pray. On one occasion I heard an old teaching of his on prayer. What he said has been forever etched into my heart and has affected the way I spend time with God. Here's what he said, in essence:

> Learn to wait on the Lord the way an eagle soars. Have you ever seen an eagle soar? It's effortless. Just before an eagle takes off, it

perches itself upon the rock near the waters and waits. It waits for the current of the wind. And because of its discerning eyes, it waits for the gentle blowing and then opens up its wings and yields to the wind. It flaps here a little and there a little, and then before you know it, brother, that thing is soaring! That's how to pray!

Few wait before God's presence because it's uncomfortable. We don't know what to do. Our minds become flooded with distractions. We don't see the value in waiting because we don't see the benefits right away. But I believe God wants to transition you into a deeper walk with Him through waiting. The more you wait before the Lord, the more the weight of God's glory will be seen in you. There are promises throughout the Word of God that speak on waiting before Him, and I want us to really think about what the Scriptures are saying as it relates to waiting.

Waiting before God has many powerful benefits. Consider Isaiah 40:28–31:

> Have you not known? Have you not heard? The everlasting God, the LORD, the Creator of the ends of the earth, neither faints nor is weary. His understanding is unsearchable. He gives power to the weak, and to those who have no might He increases strength. Even

the youths shall faint and be weary, and the young men shall utterly fall, but those who wait on the LORD shall renew their strength; they shall mount up with wings like eagles, they shall run and not be weary, they shall walk and not faint.

I want to walk us through this passage verse by verse. In this prophetic declaration Isaiah asks, "Have you not known?" Why did he ask that? Because there is a tendency in the human heart to forget, so we need to be reminded. The prophet went on to say, "Have you not heard? The everlasting God, the LORD..." (Isa. 40:28).

Let's pause there. The word "everlasting" in that verse means perpetual or without end.[1] It tells us He is an unending fountain of eternal life. Also notice that "LORD" is in small capital letters. That tells us the scripture is referring to Yahweh or Jehovah, God's personal name.

The passage continues, "The Creator of the ends of the earth, neither faints nor is weary" (Isa. 40:28). The Lord never ceases. He is constant. "His understanding is unsearchable" (Isa. 40:28). You cannot fully grasp His understanding. I once heard a man of God say, "The moment you understand God, you cease to know Him." To *understand* means you're standing over something, so it's *under your standing.* So many times in our walk with the Lord, we want to understand things. We want to know things with our earthly mental capacity. But God's understanding is truly unsearchable.

Verse 29 says, "He gives power to the weak" (Isa. 40). *Power* means ability and strength,[2] so here we read that God gives power, ability, and strength to the weak. If you feel as if you have power over yourself, you receive no power, because power does not come from us. Power comes from God, and His power is invested in the weak.

Something happens when you rely on the Lord and acknowledge your weakness. Paul said, "I will all the more gladly boast in my weaknesses, so that the power of Christ [may completely enfold me and] may dwell in me...for when I am weak [in human strength], then I am strong [truly able, truly powerful, truly drawing from God's strength]" (2 Cor. 12:9–10, AMP). It's not a false humility that says, "Oh, look at me; I'm weak." Rather, it's a true discernment of who you are—that you have nothing in yourself. This is why Jesus says, "For without Me you can do nothing" (John 15:5). We too must realize this.

The power of God is given to the weak. Those who truly understand their limitations and frailties know their weakness is something to boast in because it is precisely in weakness that we have power. In weakness we have strength. Now, this is not a weakness like sin—I'm not excusing sin. What

I'm talking about is our frailties and our limitations. Don't use Scripture to accommodate a life of rebellion toward the Lord or think, "Oh, I'm always going to struggle with this. It's my weakness." The devil is a liar! God did not call you to carry something He conquered on the cross. The weakness I'm referring to is our need for Him. We don't have strength in ourselves.

Do you want to walk holy before the Lord? Give your life to Him. Everything is found in His presence. The strength you need, the fruit of the Holy Spirit in your life, the self-control, the freedom from bondage you seek—it's all found in Him. The Lord does not want you to walk around full of sin, bondage, and addictions. That is not your portion. The Lord wants to give you power—power over the devil and over your flesh.

We give the devil too much credit and authority in our lives. We give him a crown that is undue. Many times we blame the devil when the issue is our flesh. The Holy Spirit wants to give you power, but He gives power to the weak and those who know they are in need of Him. I once heard a man of God say, "The Lord will never turn empty those who are hungry, except those who are full of themselves."

Continuing in Isaiah 40, verse 30 says, "Even the youths shall faint and be weary, and the young men shall utterly fall." Youths are known for strength, vigor, and vitality, right? But Isaiah says in the next verse, "But those who wait on the LORD shall renew their strength; they shall mount up with wings like eagles, they shall run and not be weary, they shall walk and not faint." Power, strength, and renewal come in the waiting. Notice "LORD" is in small capitals again. That means God's personal name is being used. So we hear the Lord saying that when we wait on Him, we're waiting on a God who is personal. He gives us His name, Yahweh. When you want to invite someone into a closer relationship with you, you allow them to call you by your first name. This is what God is doing here. He is speaking to us with the intimacy that comes through relationship.

In Genesis 1:1 God is referred to as Elohim, the Creator. But in Genesis chapter 2 after God makes man, He is called by His personal name: Yahweh or Jehovah (or Yehovah), the great I Am. (See Genesis 2:8.) What does that reveal? That man was created to be intimate with a personal God. The great "I Am That I Am" (Exod. 3:14, KJV) wants us to know Him not just as Creator but *intimately* as our Lord who is always with us.

Again Isaiah 40:31 says that "those who wait on the LORD shall renew their strength." To renew something means to make it new again. You see, in God's presence His mercies are new. In God's presence everything is constantly fresh. The promise to those who wait on the Lord is that their strength will be renewed. And He says, "They shall mount up with wings like eagles" (Isa. 40:31).

If you've never seen an eagle soaring, let me tell you, it's breathtaking! Not long ago my wife and I were walking on a trail, and we saw an enormous eagle. It was soaring high in the sky, but it wasn't flapping its wings. It was simply gliding, taken over by the current of the wind. That's what eagles do. They perch on a rock or a tree, discern the wind, and then mount up and yield to it. They flap their wings for a bit, but the next thing you know, they're soaring.

That is what it's like to wait before the Lord. We perch on the Rock of Ages, resting in His nearness, and wait to sense the wind of His Spirit. As we yield to the wind of God's Spirit, we are overtaken by His presence, and in that place we gain renewed strength.

THE PROMISE TO THOSE WHO WAIT ON THE LORD IS THAT THEIR STRENGTH WILL BE RENEWED.

Isaiah says that in waiting, not only will you renew your strength and not only will you "mount up with wings like eagles," but you will "run and not be weary" (40:31). You will get a boost from a new fuel source called *grace*. As you are energized in the presence and glory of God, you will walk and not faint. You are given supernatural strength, supernatural renewal.

When many of us think of waiting, our minds go to times when we waited for God to do something particular or for a season to pass. We say things like, "Just wait on the Lord, brother. This too will pass." Yes, there are seasons of waiting for situations to change. Yes, we must wait for God's timing. But there is another kind of waiting on the Lord.

"Wait" in Isaiah 40:30 is the Hebrew word *qāvâ*. It means "to wait, look for, hope, expect," but it also means to twist, as with a rope.[3] The more you spend time waiting before the Lord, not looking for anything in particular but just being with Him, there is a twisting of the fiber of your spirit with His Spirit so they are intertwined as one. As the apostle Paul proclaimed, "He who is joined to the Lord is one spirit with Him" (1 Cor. 6:17). And then strength is given.

PRACTICING STILLNESS

This is what it looks like to truly wait on the Lord. First, you find a time to be alone. The best time is when you're the most rested. For some that is early in the morning. Maybe for you it's in the afternoon. Or perhaps it's late at night when everyone else is in bed.

You must find a time when your soul is the quietest, when your thoughts are less distracted. For me it's early morning because I've just woken up; I have no worries because the day has just begun. Maybe the Lord is calling you to do that. If you yield to Him in this way, it will be easier to connect with the Holy Spirit because there won't be many distractions.

Some people wake up and immediately grab their phones. I've been there, and what ends up happening is that you get sucked into a vortex of distractions—then you wonder why it's very diffi-cult for you to press in to God's presence. Well, it's because you've filled your mind with all the stimuli and all the news. The distraction could be anything. It doesn't have to be your phone. So I encourage you to put everything away when you spend time with the Lord. Find a time when you can be alone and rest because that's where God is—in the rest.

Second, be still. That's what it means to wait! Now, don't get discouraged when this doesn't come easily. You're learning. You may find you can be still for the first fifteen seconds, but then your thoughts start to wander. If this happens, begin to magnify the Lord. Just say something like, "Jesus, I worship You." Open your mouth and praise Him. Then get quiet again. Then go back to magnifying Him by saying, "Lord Jesus, I worship You. Father, I just come before You." Then get still again. This is how you learn to be with Him.

At first it may seem as if you're going through

this cycle every five seconds. That's OK! Stillness does not come immediately; it is something you must practice. Just as you practice prayer, you practice His presence. As you practice stillness, you go from being still for fifteen seconds to five minutes, and then longer. It's not about the quantity but the *quality* of the time spent waiting before the Lord. Often we get caught up in asking God to meet our needs, and we miss what God is really trying to do, which always comes in the stillness.

So again, first get secluded and find a time when you're most rested. Then begin with praise. Elevate the Lord and magnify Him. If you don't, you will begin to magnify other voices without even realizing it. For example, if you don't begin your prayer time with praise, you're going to think, "Man, I don't feel this," "I don't feel the Lord," or, "I feel bored." That's because you're magnifying your flesh. You're magnifying your other cares. You can't do that.

So begin with praise. Praise is not limited to a song. Praise is lifting your attention to the Lord. That gets easier to do with time. You'll realize how easy it is and how difficult we make it. As you begin to magnify the Lord, you'll become still. You'll enter rest, and entering rest is waiting before the Lord. We don't wait until God shows up. God's presence is always with us. We're waiting to get our stuff in order. Until we get to a place where we're still, our awareness of God's presence is diminished. He's waiting for us—that's why we must wait on Him.

It's easy to allow our feelings, or the lack thereof, to dictate what we think God is like. We're not meant to be led by our feelings. To those who say, "I don't feel God; He's not here," I say, "It's not that He's not there. It's that you must be still and quiet." Others say, "I feel oppressed." To that I say, "You may feel oppressed. You may feel a heaviness. You may feel a burden, but you need to lose sight of yourself and look to Him." You cannot look at the Lord and yourself at the same time. You have to look to Him. That is what waiting is!

I woke up one morning after having a very unusual night. I sensed some spiritual warfare and felt a heavy weight of oppression the enemy was trying to throw at me. Now, I'm making myself vulnerable in telling this story, but in my weakness I pray you'll find the glory of God. I want my story to refresh and encourage you to believe that God can do the same for you.

So this morning was just very strange. I woke up feeling this resistance, this spiritual warfare. I had a decision to make. Would I grab my phone or grab the Word? Would I go back to sleep or spend time with the Lord? I chose to get up, get a cup of coffee, grab my Bible, go to the living room, and sit with the Lord. I could have started binding the spirit of this and that, but I didn't do that because by doing so, I would have ended up magnifying the enemy.

YOU HAVE TO LOOK TO HIM.
THAT IS WHAT WAITING IS!

Now, I'm not against rebuking the enemy. What I'm saying is that you don't want to open your day by giving the enemy any breathing space. Don't give him any of your attention. Give God all your attention!

As I sat in my living room, all this oppression came. So I began to say, "I worship You, Lord." I thought about the fact that all things are under Jesus' feet and He disarmed all principalities and powers on the cross, and I opened my mouth and began to thank the Lord that I didn't "feel" anything. But in that moment I took my eyes off myself and put them back on the Lord. I started worshipping Him, at first lifting my hands, and then just being still, praying and praising quietly in the Spirit. You can do this because stillness is a matter of the heart.

As I offered myself to the Lord and lifted Him up, all those thoughts—the oppression, the distracting thoughts, the overt self-awareness—began to dissipate. As I sat there waiting on the Lord, I was renewed. I had an awareness of God's presence, a heightened sense of His glory, and a beautiful strength from the Holy Spirit. All this happened because I chose to go into the presence of God, letting go of all my cares and concerns and lifting Him alone. When we do that, God renews us.

There are two types of Christians: soulish Christians and spiritual Christians. Soulish Christians are led by their souls—their minds, wills, and emotions. Spiritual Christians are led by their spirits, the part of us that is connected to the Spirit of God. Soulish Christians lean on their understanding. They're led by their emotions. Spiritual Christians disregard their own feelings and thoughts and put their attention on the Lord. The spiritual Christian still battles the soul, but soulish Christians magnify the soul. They magnify their thoughts and cares. Spiritual Christians, on the other hand, are led not by what they feel but by the One in whom they believe.

In 1 Thessalonians 5:23 Paul says, "May your whole spirit, soul, and body be preserved blameless at the coming of our Lord Jesus Christ." Paul presents a beautiful mystery here, again showing us that we are spirit, soul, and body. As we discussed in chapter 2, as believers, we must prioritize the spiritual above our own souls, above our own feelings, and above our own bodies. When we prioritize the spirit, the soul and body align with it.

When you bypass all the fluff and soulish stuff, you connect spirit to Spirit. As you do, your soul will be illumined by the peace and light of God's Spirit. Your mind, will, and emotions will be subjugated to your spirit so your spirit has dominance over your soul. When you live like this, you begin to have the mind of Christ. You think His thoughts. His will becomes your will, your emotions align with His emotions, and your soul becomes a conduit of His character.

If you want to get close to the Lord, then you must learn to disregard yourself. Jesus said, "If anyone desires to come after Me, let him deny himself, and take up his cross, and follow Me" (Matt. 16:24). Serving the Lord is about keeping your eyes on Him and losing sight of yourself. If you lose sight of yourself, you will find true life. But if you're holding on to your own will, thoughts, and feelings, you will lose. If you let go of all that, you'll begin to operate under a higher grace. That's what God wants. Too many believers are magnifying their own thoughts and the deceits of the devil. We have to get past ourselves to connect with God, spirit to Spirit.

Let's look at Isaiah 40:29–31 again:

> He gives power to the weak, and to those who have no might He increases strength. Even the youths shall faint and be weary, and the young men shall utterly fall, but those who wait on the LORD shall renew their strength.

You may say, "Yes, I'm waiting on the Lord, but I'm not really receiving the renewal I need." That just means you're not done waiting on Him.

It is impossible for God to lie. Again, Isaiah 40 says, "Those who wait on the Lord *shall* renew their strength" (v. 31, emphasis added). It doesn't say He *might*. "They shall mount up with wings like eagles, they shall run and not be weary, they shall walk and not faint" (Isa. 40:31). The reason you think you're not being renewed as you wait on the Lord is that the cares, distractions, woes, and worries of life have your attention instead of the Lord.

WAITING BRINGS REST

The Hebrew word translated "wait" also means to "look for, hope, expect."[4] When we wait on the Lord, we have an expectation. We are looking for Him. We are eager to linger in God's presence. To linger is "to be slow in parting or in quitting something."[5] When we linger, we stay in a place longer than necessary because we are reluctant to leave. God invites us to linger—to be slow, even reluctant, to leave His presence. He wants to lead us to a place of rest.

If you like to work out, you know it is just as important to rest as it is to strength train. Guys who like to grow their muscles at the gym will often tell you that rest is tied to muscle recovery. So when you're working out, you need a set time to rest because the muscle growth is as much in the place of rest as in the place of pressing (weight lifting). Strength and recovery are tied to waiting, as is freedom.

In Leviticus 25 we read about the year of Jubilee.

> And you shall count seven sabbaths of years for yourself, seven times seven years; and the time of the seven sabbaths of years shall be to you forty-nine years. Then you shall cause the trumpet of the Jubilee to sound on the tenth day of the seventh month; on the Day of Atonement you shall make the trumpet to sound throughout all your land. And you shall consecrate the fiftieth year, and proclaim liberty throughout all the land to all its inhabitants. It shall be a Jubilee for you; and each of you shall return to his possession, and each of you shall return to his family. That fiftieth year shall be a Jubilee to you; in it you shall neither sow nor reap what grows of its own accord, nor gather the grapes of your untended vine. For it is the Jubilee; it shall be holy to you; you shall eat its produce from the field.
>
> —LEVITICUS 25:8–12

The Jubilee year was tied to rest. There was to be no work. But it was also a year of freedom and of debts being cleared. Genesis 49:18 says, "I have waited for your salvation, O LORD!" Again, rest is tied to waiting, and waiting is tied to *regaining*.

HE WANTS TO LEAD US
TO A PLACE OF REST.

God lives in rest. When we wait upon the Lord, we enter a spiritual Jubilee rest, where we recover, gain strength, and are renewed and revived. We enter a place of liberty we've never known because we come into restful state with God, who dwells in rest. Waiting brings about true rest.

Exodus 33:13–15 (AMP, emphasis added) tells us:

"Now therefore, I pray you, if I have found favor in Your sight, let me know Your ways so that I may know You [becoming more deeply and intimately acquainted with You, recognizing and understanding Your ways more clearly] and that I may find grace and favor in Your sight. And consider also, that this nation is Your people." And the LORD said, "My presence shall go with you, and *I will give you rest* [by bringing you and the people into the promised land]." And Moses said to Him, "If Your presence does not go [with me], do not lead us up from here. For how then can it be known that Your people and I have found favor in Your sight? Is it not by Your going with us, so that we are distinguished, Your people and I, from all the [other] people on the face of the earth?"

God says, "My presence will go with you, and you will find rest." The children of Israel were once enslaved. They were in bondage for four hundred years; then the presence of God brought them rest, carrying them from Egypt through the wilderness and eventually to the Promised Land. That was also a Jubilee. Remember, after "seven sabbaths of years... seven times seven" (forty-nine years), the slaves would be free (in the fiftieth year) (Lev. 25:8–12).

The presence of God is still bringing rest and renewal as He leads His children out of slavery and into freedom. Much like the people of Israel, we who were once enslaved to sin have been led by the Spirit of God out of that captivity and given rest.

Psalm 27:14 charges us to "be of good courage, and He shall strengthen your heart; wait, I say, on the LORD!" So not only does waiting provide renewal, rest, and recovery, but it also strengthens the heart. Why wouldn't we want to wait upon the Lord in prayer?

WAITING IS NECESSARY

Waiting on God has become a lost art. Why? Because we live in a microwave generation, an age of instant gratification. We want everything right now. But God is not focused on doing things quickly. When it comes to prayer, the posture of our hearts should be one of patient waiting and expectation.

There are similarities between spiritual and natural things. If you were to microwave a steak for five to ten minutes, it would cook, but it would taste terrible. Why? Because the cook time was rushed. There was no time to let the meat marinate and cook slowly so it could get tender. Microwaving skips the processes that would make steak juicy and flavorful.

Waiting on the Lord is like taking the time to marinate and properly cook a steak. When something is marinated or slow-cooked, it tastes better. It has a richer flavor. That's how it is with the Lord. When we take the time to wait on the Lord, lingering in His presence, a deep enrichment—a deep "flavor"—comes upon our lives in prayer. This is why waiting should be part of your daily communion with the Holy Spirit, because it brings greater clarity, strength, and renewal. It brings you to a place of rest instead of frustration, and both your posture and your outlook will be different because you're spending time marinating in the things of God.

Do not rush the Holy Spirit in prayer. Do not rush through your time with the Lord. I'm convinced that when we enjoy the process of lingering, when we enjoy waiting and just being with the Lord, that itself becomes an answer to many of our prayers. "Marinating" takes place in the Spirit, and we gain a perspective that comes only from our time in His presence.

Many times the answer we seek comes in the midst of waiting. In those moments, we experience the weight of God's presence—and in the weight of God's presence the heart is strengthened, revived, and renewed. You may be thinking, "But I thought the heart is desperately wicked. Who can know it?" Jeremiah 17:9 does say that, but that is not the last word on our hearts. Scripture also says later in Jeremiah:

> Behold, the days are coming, says the LORD, when I will make a new covenant with the house of Israel and with the house of Judah—not according to the covenant that I made with their fathers in the day that I took them by the hand to lead them out of the land of Egypt, My covenant which they broke, though I was a husband to them, says the LORD. But this is the covenant that I will make with the house of Israel after those days, says the LORD: I will put My law in their minds, and write it on their hearts; and I will be their God, and they shall be My people. No more shall every man teach his neighbor, and every man his brother, saying, "Know the LORD," for they all shall know Me, from the least of them to the greatest of them, says the LORD. For I will forgive their iniquity, and their sin I will remember no more.
>
> —JEREMIAH 31:31-34

We also read in Ezekiel 11:19–20:

> Then I will give them one heart, and I will put
> a new spirit within them, and take the stony
> heart out of their flesh, and give them a heart
> of flesh, that they may walk in My statutes and
> keep My judgments and do them; and they
> shall be My people, and I will be their God.

Both Jeremiah and Ezekiel speak of us receiving a new, born-again nature that is sensitive to the things of God.

I encourage you to spend as much time as you can waiting before the Lord in prayer. Before you ask God for anything, posture your heart to wait. This is thoroughly scriptural. Jesus tells us to ask, seek, and knock (Matt. 7:7). There is a time for asking and bringing our petitions before the Lord. But there is also a time for seeking—a time of waiting on the Lord, enjoying moments with Him, loving Him for who He is, and praising Him because He's worthy. Waiting is a decision to yield to the Lord instead of taking control for yourself. When you wait on the Lord, you're saying, "I give up control, and I rest in You." So before you ask, before you knock, let there be a time of seeking, a time of expectation in His presence, and a time to marinate and sensitize your heart.

WAITING IS A WEAPON

Waiting is tied to true warfare—it is a weapon and a posture of faith. Many mighty people of God had lives of waiting. Moses waited. Joshua waited. David waited. Jehoshaphat waited. They all gave up control and just waited to be led by God's holy presence.

We too must wait on the Lord. In Matthew 11:28–29 Jesus says, "Come to Me, all you who labor and are heavy laden, and I will give you rest. Take My yoke upon you and learn from Me, for I am gentle and lowly in heart, and you will find rest for your souls." Notice in that passage, all you need to do is come to the Lord. He will do the rest as you take on His yoke and wait on Him. Habakkuk 2:1 says, "I will stand my watch and set myself on the rampart, and watch to see what He will say to me, and what I will answer when I am corrected." The prophet Habakkuk chose to patiently stand on the watch, and he received guidance.

Again, to wait means to linger. Learn to wait on the Lord. When you're praying, don't rush in the presence of the Lord. Many times we think we're supposed to wait until God shows up. No, we're waiting until *we* show up. God is already there. God is omnipresent. What happens is that *we're* not present. We're distracted and burdened with the cares of life. So when we spend time with God, the majority of our time should be spent waiting before His presence. Waiting gets you into a posture of rest and recovery. Stay there!

Free your mind from striving and trying to make something happen. God's Spirit is already present. When you wait, when you linger in God's presence, the layers of your own strivings come to an end and you reach the end of yourself. When you reach the end of yourself, you gain Him. You see Him because you're decreasing, and He is increasing.

ALL YOU NEED TO DO IS COME TO THE LORD. HE WILL DO THE REST.

Rest in the finished work of Christ and cast all your cares on Him. Worrying will do nothing, but waiting will align your heart to His. Whatever your worries and concerns, whatever is holding you back, in whatever ways you're striving, whatever you're magnifying—rest in the finished work of Jesus. His yoke is easy, and His burden is light. He will give you rest for your soul as you wait in His presence.

Let's pray:

> *Lord God, teach us to patiently wait in Your presence, knowing strength, rest, and renewal are in the waiting. Lord, we're not waiting for You to show up. You're waiting for us to show up. Help us be attentive to*

You, to enjoy the time spent with You, to linger in Your presence, to stay a while, and to spend quality time with You. We thank You, Father, for completing that work in us. Help us to never rush Your Spirit—to never rush Your presence.

Father, we thank You for doing this mighty work in us for Your glory. In the name of Jesus, amen.

POINTS TO PONDER

- Waiting upon the Lord renews and refreshes me.

- I am like an eagle designed to soar on the wind of God's presence.

- I must learn the art of waiting, embracing my weaknesses and depending upon God.

- I will not be discouraged if I don't receive anything in my waiting with the Lord. It's a process and time spent well.

For answers to some common questions about waiting on the Lord, see the appendix.

Chapter 5

THE FIFTH SECRET: GETTING STILL TO HEAR

ENJOY PLAYING THE guitar from time to time. In fact when I first met my wife, we spent our first couple of dates worshipping and praising the Lord together as I played the guitar. If you're a guitar player, you know that shifts in weather, such as too much or too little humidity, can affect your guitar. The strings either get too tight or too loose, and the guitar goes out of tune. Often you end up having to put the guitar on your lap and tune each string to the right tone because if the strings are out of tune, they'll be out of sync with the notes you want to play.

This is very similar to how we hear the Lord. The strings of our hearts often get weathered by the noise and circumstances of life, and we get out of tune, or out of sync, with the tone of the Spirit. But God doesn't want us to stay this way; He wants to bring us in tune, or in harmony, with the sound of the Spirit through His presence and Word.

Harmony is "the combination of simultaneously sounded musical notes to produce chords and chord progressions having a pleasing effect."[1] That's the musical definition of harmony. But the more fundamental definition can be summed up with one word: agreement. Harmony is an agreement of ideas, feelings, or actions, or a pleasing combination of different parts. To be in harmony with the Holy Spirit is to be in agreement with His ideas, feelings, and actions.

HARMONY THROUGH COMMUNION

Do you want to hear the sound of the Spirit, the voice of the Lord, in your life? Then first and foremost you must know that He has called you to a life of communion. How can you hear the Spirit if you're not in communion with Him? Communion is "the sharing or exchanging of intimate thoughts and feelings, especially when the exchange is on a mental or spiritual level."[2] To commune with someone is to share their thoughts. It is an intimate expression. Communion is not something shared between acquaintances. It comes from two words: commune, which is to have a relationship, and union, which is oneness. It is in communion that God shares His thoughts; therefore, it is the way to hear from Him.

It is very important to understand that God has called *you* to a life of communion. He designed mankind to be in relationship with Him. Genesis 1:26 says, "Let Us make man in Our image, according to Our likeness." God is obviously much bigger than we can comprehend. But because we are made in His image and likeness, we have the capacity to be in a relationship with Him and commune with Him. A relationship is "the way in which two or more concepts, objects, or people are connected, or the state of being connected."[3] The reality is that you are called to be connected to the Spirit; you are called to communion with Him. You are called to share the thoughts, feelings, and purposes of His heart on a deep, personal, and spiritual level because the Spirit of God is inside you.

REVELATION THROUGH COMMUNION

In the first letter to the Corinthians, Paul wrote:

> What eye has not seen and ear has not heard and has not entered into the heart of man, [all that] God has prepared (made and keeps ready) for those who love Him [who hold Him in affectionate reverence, promptly obeying Him and gratefully recognizing the benefits He has bestowed]. Yet to us God has unveiled and revealed them by and through His Spirit.
> —1 CORINTHIANS 2:9–10, AMPC

Paul is speaking to us—to the believer, the child of God. And he's saying none of us have ever been able to comprehend the things of God.

He continues:

> For the [Holy] Spirit searches diligently, exploring and examining everything, even sounding the profound and bottomless things of God [the divine counsels and things hidden and beyond man's scrutiny]. For what person perceives (knows and understands) what passes through a man's thoughts except the man's own spirit within him? Just so no one discerns (comes to know and comprehend) the thoughts of God except the Spirit of God.
>
> —1 CORINTHIANS 2:10–11, AMPC

So here Paul makes the point that no one can fully know a person's thoughts and who that person truly is except for that person. In the same way, no one can understand the ways and thoughts of God's Spirit except the Spirit of God Himself.

Paul then says, "We have not received the spirit [that belongs to] the world, but the [Holy] Spirit Who is from God, [given to us] that we might realize and comprehend and appreciate the gifts [of divine favor and blessing so freely and lavishly] bestowed on us by God" (1 Cor. 2:12, AMPC).

No one can comprehend God's thoughts except His Spirit, but the reality is that you and I have received His Spirit, and we can freely receive all that God has given. If you are in Jesus, God's Spirit resides in you and He wants to reveal the deep things of the Spirit to your spirit.

God wants to unveil by His Spirit "[all that] God has prepared (made and keeps ready) for those who love Him" (1 Cor. 2:9, AMPC). That's a beautiful reality—a promise you can lay hold of through communion.

ONENESS WITH THE HOLY SPIRIT

Paul goes on to say in 1 Corinthians 2:13 (AMP):

> We also speak of these things, not in words taught or supplied by human wisdom, but in those taught by the Spirit, combining and interpreting spiritual thoughts with spiritual words [for those being guided by the Holy Spirit].

How does the Holy Spirit speak to us? He teaches those who have His Spirit within and are led by Him by combining and interpreting spiritual truths with spiritual language. The Holy Spirit never speaks outside of truth, which is the Word of God. The Bible tells us, again, that there are three that agree in heaven—the Father, the Word, and the Spirit. These three are one.

The Spirit of God will often combine and interpret

the spiritual truths of the Word of God, and He will give us spiritual language from the Word to reveal what He is speaking to us through the Word. In other words, the Holy Spirit is the revealer of God's Word. When you don't understand something, He will unveil it and will give language to the written Word in a way that you can understand and apply. (See 1 Corinthians 2:12–13.) That promise is given to those who possess the Holy Spirit and are guided by Him. Are you in Jesus? Have you received the gift of salvation? Have you freely received His grace? Then you have the Spirit of God dwelling inside you.

Let's continue to look at 1 Corinthians 2. Verse 14 says, "But the natural, nonspiritual man does not accept or welcome or admit into his heart the gifts and teachings and revelations of the Spirit of God, for they are folly...to him" (AMPC). Put another way, the gifts, teachings, and revelations of the Spirit are nonsensical and meaningless to him because that person is naturally minded.

Naturally minded people live by the dictates of their five physical senses. Their outlooks are completely carnal and not influenced by the Spirit. They see only the natural order of things, and that mentality is at enmity with God. They can never welcome into their hearts the gifts, teachings, and revelations of the Spirit because they cannot understand the things of the Spirit.

Paul goes on to say in verse 14, "He is incapable

of knowing them [of progressively recognizing, understanding, and becoming better acquainted with them] because they are spiritually discerned and estimated and appreciated" (AMPC). You see, because we have the Holy Spirit in us, because we are born again, we now have the capacity to discern and appreciate the things of the Spirit. God wants us to know what He has freely given to us. He wants us to hear from Him.

UNDERSTANDING THE MIND OF CHRIST

First Corinthians 2 closes with verse 16 (AMPC), saying:

> For who has known or understood the mind (the counsels and purposes) of the Lord so as to guide and instruct Him and give Him knowledge? But we have the mind of Christ (the Messiah) and do hold the thoughts (feelings and purposes) of His heart.

The reality is that you have the mind of Jesus. You hold the thoughts, feelings, and purposes of His heart.

Notice also the word *mind* in this verse. Our fellowship with God helps us make decisions. How? The oneness created in our communion, or harmony, with God transmits to us the thoughts—the mind—of Christ. The Spirit of God is in you, wants to guide your steps, and wants to reveal the deep things in the Word to you; He does this through communion. Communion is to have a relationship; it is to share life. It is a sweet exchange.

Remember what we saw earlier—the definition of communion is the exchange of thoughts and feelings on an intimate level. That is what happens when you commune with God. There is a sharing of thoughts and feelings on a very deep and personal level. You will find yourself receiving revelation from the Word, and you will see the Scriptures in light of the breath and inspiration of the Holy Spirit. You will begin to have His thoughts and exhibit the fruit of His Spirit. You will be in tune, in harmony, and in cadence with the Spirit by communing with Him.

This is a wonderful reality—the Spirit of God wants to speak with you and reveal His heart and mind to you! But how does He speak to us? I want to point out five primary ways God's Spirit communicates with us.

FIVE WAYS GOD SPEAKS TO US

1. The Word of God

The first and most important way God speaks is through His Word. This is why it's so important that we prioritize reading and meditating on Scripture.

How can you hear what God sounds like if you're not reading what He has said? How can you discern what's of God and what's of the flesh if you're not familiar with His Word?

Many people overlook a critical truth about Scripture. Hebrews 4:12 says, "For the Word that God *speaks* is *alive* and *full of power* [making it active, operative, energizing, and effective]; it is sharper than any two-edged sword" (AMPC, emphasis added). This is what the Word of God does—it "speaks" and "is alive and full of power [making it active, operative, energizing, and effective]." The Word has power in and of itself.

Hebrews 4:12 (AMPC) goes on to say,

> It is sharper than any two-edged sword, penetrating to the dividing line of the breath of life (soul) and [the immortal] spirit, and of joints and marrow [of the deepest parts of our nature], exposing and sifting and analyzing and judging the very thoughts and purposes of the heart.

God's Word is energizing and sharper than a two-edged sword, having the divine ability to separate soul and spirit, joint and marrow—the very thoughts and intentions of the heart. Just as it is nearly impossible to divide the bone from the marrow, so it is with dividing the thoughts of the mind and the intentions of the heart, or the soul and the spirit. You cannot do that on your own but would need a supernatural influence.

This is exactly what the Word of God is. It is the only influence that has the ability to cut that deeply and profoundly. It's able to divide the joint and marrow. The Word is able to separate the soul— your mind, will, and emotions, the emotional part of you—from the spirit, which is the part where the Spirit of God resides. When you prioritize studying and meditating on the Word, it will cut you. When you analyze the Word, it will analyze you. The Word will reveal what's really in you.

The greatest way to discern the voice of the Holy Spirit is through the Word of God because the Holy Spirit will use it to expose and sift what is truly Him from what is just you. It is tremendously effective at distinguishing God's voice from your own.

Let me make this practical. Perhaps someone thinks, "God has left me, because I cannot hear Him anymore." We can discern that is a lie because Hebrews 13:5 says God will never leave us or forsake us. The Word of God exposes that thought as a fleshly, soulish response to His desire.

**WHEN YOU ANALYZE THE
WORD, IT WILL ANALYZE YOU.**

Now, remember that I said we must harmonize with the Spirit through communion. Harmony is agreement. When we prioritize the Word of God, we come into harmony, into agreement, with what He says. When we purpose in our hearts to agree with God's Word, we will receive that which He speaks to us.

So the primary, most effective way God will speak to us is through His Word because it is sharp and exposes our true intentions. There is no way, other than the Word of God, to effectively discern what comes from the spirit versus the soul.

2. Prayer

Another way the Holy Spirit will speak to us is through prayer. Charles Spurgeon once said: "When asked, 'What is more important: Prayer or Reading the Bible?' I ask, 'What is more important: Breathing in or Breathing out?'"[4] His point was that both are equally important. You must live by breathing in the Word of God and breathing out prayer. You need both.

Prayer causes you to be in tune with the Spirit. Going back to my guitar example from the beginning of this chapter, when I lay my guitar on my lap to tune it, the guitar doesn't need to do anything. It does not need to worry about anything. It is my responsibility to tune it. The guitar's only job is to rest on my lap. In the same way, if we wait on the Lord and rest in His presence, His Spirit will tune our hearts to hear what He's saying. We don't have to strive or try to force God to speak. That is His job. He will tune you to capture the tone of the Spirit. Your responsibility is to present yourself before Him—to be in prayer and fellowship with the Lord.

Psalm 46:10 says, "Be still, and know that I am God; I will be exalted among the nations, I will be exalted in the earth!" When we are still, the "knowing" will come. When we are still, the mind of Christ becomes elevated in our spirits. When we are still, fleshly impulses and all the noise and distractions begin to subside. Our thoughts become His thoughts. Our feelings become His feelings. What grieves Him grieves us. What gives Him joy brings us joy. What God loves we begin to love. What God hates we begin to hate. And it's all because of that union of prayer.

You see, prayer prepares your heart to receive the Word of God. I encourage you to prayerfully read the Word. Don't just read it for the sake of reading it or as a chore. Read it prayerfully, and your heavenly Father will reveal the Word to you in a way that is truly life-changing. The Word will become energized in your spirit.

So the second way to hear from God is to live a life of prayer. But you must also surrender, or yield, to Him. It's not about trying to force anything. A life of prayer is a life of yielding, surrender, and rest. Be still and know that He is God. He will be exalted in the nations.

3. Spiritual gifts

A third way God can speak to you is through spiritual gifts. In 1 Corinthians 12 we see that there are many gifts of the Holy Spirit.

> But the manifestation of the Spirit is given to each one for the profit of all: for to one is given the word of wisdom through the Spirit, to another the word of knowledge through the same Spirit, to another faith by the same Spirit, to another gifts of healings by the same Spirit, to another the working of miracles, to another prophecy, to another discerning of spirits, to another different kinds of tongues, to another the interpretation of tongues. But one and the same Spirit works all these things, distributing to each one individually as He wills.
>
> —1 CORINTHIANS 12:7–11

There are three revelatory, or "seeing," gifts: word of knowledge, word of wisdom, and discerning of spirits. There are three gifts of power: faith, miracles, and healings (note that's *healings*, plural). And there are three "speaking" gifts: tongues, the interpretation of tongues, and prophecy. If you are sensitive enough, perhaps you will be able to hear the Lord's voice through one of these spiritual gifts. However, we must test *all* things to make sure everything we hear aligns with the Word of God. This is why I say the primary and most effective way to hear God is through Scripture, followed by prayer, *then* spiritual gifts.

Years ago I was in a situation and desperately needed to hear from God. During that season an elder from our church approached me in private and reached out to hug me. Then he began to speak in other tongues. By the grace of the Holy Spirit, I understood those tongues as if they were a known language, and they were exactly what I needed to hear at that moment.

There was another time when I ran away from the Lord. My heart began to harden, and I stopped fellowshipping with the Lord. I was burdened by so many trials. I felt defeated. I was living with my grandmother at the time, and one day early in the morning I heard her praying and sobbing uncontrollably. I was about to leave my room when the Spirit of God spoke to my spirit and said, "You sit down because I'm going to speak to you right now."

My grandmother was praying in other tongues in her room, and when I sat down on my bed, she opened the door with great urgency and exclaimed in a loud voice, "My son, why have you forsaken Me? Why have you abandoned Me? Don't you know that

I have a good plan for you? Don't you know that I have a purpose for your life? But you cannot receive the blessing if you're not in communion with Me. Now repent and turn back to Me."

I *knew* that was God. My grandmother had no idea I had fallen away from the Lord. But I felt the conviction of the Holy Spirit, and that day I was gloriously delivered from so many bondages. You see, God spoke to me through my grandmother using a spiritual gift, and God can work in your life using spiritual gifts too.

There's a wonderful story in 2 Kings 3 that also illustrates the power of spiritual gifts in hearing from God. The kings of Israel, Judah, and Edom banded together to fight the Moabites. They set out for battle with their armies and after seven days found themselves without water for themselves or their animals. The king of Israel thought God was delivering them into the hands of Moab. But Jehoshaphat, king of Judah, said, "Is there no prophet of the LORD here, that we may inquire of the LORD by him?" (2 Kings 3:11; see also verses 1–10).

They found the prophet Elisha, and the king of Israel told him they wanted to hear from God. Elisha essentially replied, "Well, I'm not going to prophesy to you." But the king of Israel said, "Please, we need to hear from God" (2 Kings 3:13, paraphrased). And Elisha said, "Were it not that I regard the presence of Jehoshaphat king of Judah, I would not look at

you, nor see you. But now bring me a musician"
(2 Kings 3:14–15). When the musician began to play,
the hand of the Lord came over Elisha, and he began
to prophesy (vv. 15–16).

God spoke to the kings using the gift of prophecy,
but Elisha needed a musician to get to a place of
communion where he could hear from the Spirit.

This reminds me of another story in Scripture. In
1 Samuel 10:1–6 the prophet Samuel approached a
man named Saul and anointed him king, saying:

> Is it not because the LORD has anointed you
> commander over His inheritance? When you
> have departed from me today, you will find
> two men by Rachel's tomb in the territory
> of Benjamin at Zelzah; and they will say to
> you, "The donkeys which you went to look
> for have been found. And now your father has
> ceased caring about the donkeys and is wor-
> rying about you, saying, 'What shall I do about
> my son?'" Then you shall go on forward from
> there and come to the terebinth tree of Tabor.
> There three men going up to God at Bethel
> will meet you, one carrying three young goats,
> another carrying three loaves of bread, and
> another carrying a skin of wine.
>
> And they will greet you and give you two
> loaves of bread, which you shall receive from
> their hands. After that you shall come to
> the hill of God where the Philistine garrison

is. And it will happen, when you have come there to the city, that you will meet a group of prophets coming down from the high place with a stringed instrument, a tambourine, a flute, and a harp before them; and they will be prophesying. Then the Spirit of the LORD will come upon you, and you will prophesy with them and be turned into another man.

When Saul left Samuel, God gave Saul a new heart, a sensitive heart. Why? Because there was a turning. This is what worship does. It turns our hearts in the Lord's direction. When Saul saw the prophets "coming down from the high place," they were praising and worshipping. There was an atmosphere of adoration, and that atmosphere was contagious. It got to Saul, and he was changed into another person. He began to prophesy. The Lord spoke to him and through him.

The same thing can happen to us today. When we go into the presence of God and we're sensitive and discerning, when we worship and praise Him, we will receive a new outlook. Our hearts will be changed, and God will begin to show us things.

Be aware that when He speaks, it is not always through words. Habakkuk 2:1 says, "I will stand my watch...to see what He will say." Habakkuk doesn't say, "I will *hear* what the Lord will say." He says he will "*see* what the Lord will say." There is a revelatory, inward vision—a spiritual gift—that the Spirit can use to enable you to hear from the Lord.

4. Peace

A fourth way God can speak to you is through peace. The Bible tells us the peace of God is able to lead us.

> And let the peace (soul harmony which comes) from Christ rule (act as umpire continually) in your hearts [deciding and settling with finality all questions that arise in your minds, in that peaceful state] to which as [members of Christ's] one body you were also called [to live]. And be thankful (appreciative), [giving praise to God always].
> —COLOSSIANS 3:15, AMPC

How does God speak to us through His peace? When anxious or negative thoughts begin to overwhelm you and you fix your attention on Christ, you'll settle into that peace, that soul harmony. Jesus said, "My peace I give to you; not as the world gives do I give to you" (John 14:27). The peace of God surpasses all human understanding. It will "guard your hearts and minds" (Phil. 4:7), but the peace of God also will settle with finality all the questions you may have.

Have you ever been in a situation where you desperately needed to hear from God? Maybe there was a crisis, a storm, an offense, or a relationship that was grieving you. In the middle of a circumstance like that, have you ever cried out to the Lord and suddenly received peace, and you just knew that everything was going to be OK? Don't dismiss that when it happens. Don't take that lightly, because that is God speaking to your spirit.

5. Confirmation

The fifth way God speaks to us is through confirmations. Let's say you're praying and reading the Word. You think the Holy Spirit may be speaking to you, and you're prayerfully considering what you heard. Then a brother or a sister comes to you and says exactly what you thought you heard, though they had no idea what was going on. That's confirmation.

God uses people to confirm His words to us, but we must not be led by confirmations, just as we are not to be led by any spiritual gift. The Bible tells us to test *all* things. We must stay focused on the Word of God. There are times when God will use a spiritual gift to speak to you. There are times when He'll use a brother or a sister to confirm something you received in prayer, but God will primarily use the Scriptures. So again, I encourage you to focus on relishing and receiving God's Word.

GET OUT OF YOUR OWN WAY

Often we allow the hands of God, instead of His face, to become our focal point. We seek His hands instead of trying to get to know and fellowship with Him. We're always trying to get something from Him. We want God to speak to us. We want to feel God in a certain way. We want to hear God in a certain way. Then we walk away untouched and frustrated. Why? Because we are preoccupied with receiving a particular touch instead of just being with Him.

Let me give you an example. One day when I was sixteen years old, I felt the Holy Spirit impressing me to fast for three days. I had been saved for about a year and had never done that before. On day one I was OK—a little tired but good. The second day, I was really tired and frustrated and I had a hard time tapping into the presence of God. The third day, I was angry and spent, so I started yelling at the Lord. I was very immature in the faith, and in my immaturity I remember telling the Lord, "Here I am fasting and seeking You, and I'm not hearing anything. I'm not seeing anything, and I'm not feeling anything. You know what? Forget it. I give up on this."

I was starting to doze off when the Holy Spirit spoke to my heart clearly: "Oh, Chris, you're seeking My hands when you should be seeking My face. Repent." I immediately knew I had to adjust my heart. I said, "Holy Spirit, forgive me. You're right. I'm sorry. I have been too preoccupied with seeking Your hands instead of Your face." As soon as I adjusted my heart, the Lord spoke very clearly to me and showed me some things that will mark me for the rest of my life. But before that word came, there had to be a heart adjustment—a simple heart repositioning.

Many times the Lord wants to give you Himself, but if you focus too much on His hands, you miss His face. When you seek His face, you will receive those hands. Again, it will often take a simple adjustment in the heart to enjoy God's presence and become finely tuned with Him. If you're the type of person who says or thinks, "You need to talk to me, God; I need to hear from You; I don't feel You," you are pushing and striving to be still.

Being still is an act of trust, of letting go. It is also an act of faith, and God is pleased with faith. He wants to speak—at the right time. He will speak to your situation at the right moment. Get to a place where the posture of your heart is simply to know Him. Don't focus too much on trying to feel or hear God. Rather, focus in prayer on getting to know the Lord intimately and enjoying His presence. Remember what communion is—the sharing of thoughts and feelings in a deep, intimate, and spiritual way. You will find that when you posture your heart for communion, you'll begin to easily discern God's will. You'll begin to easily hear from the Spirit because you're not pushing; you are just communing.

One way we often get out of touch with the Spirit is by becoming selfish. We get in our own way. Our desires, wants, cares, and concerns—we become consumed by all these things that grip us. We become *me* centered. We place all our attention on ourselves. The great I Am is God, but if we're not careful, we will replace Him with the great *me*. "I need this"; "I need that"; "Give me, give me, give me!"

BEING STILL IS AN ACT OF TRUST, OF LETTING GO.

Instead of focusing on yourself, how about giving the Lord your time? How about giving the Lord your life? How about giving Him your soul, heart, mind, and strength? How about you present yourself to Him?

FAITHFUL STILLNESS OVER FORCEFUL STRIVING

We can't make God speak to us; communication comes out of faithful stillness. Yet even those with the best intentions can find themselves forcing things in prayer and striving to get God to respond in a certain way. This happens so often that I want to address some common mistakes people make when seeking to hear God.

Looking for the mystifying

By that I mean we limit God to just a highly mystical experience. We look for the spectacular and miss the supernatural. Many times the things of the Spirit are not spectacular; they are spiritual. We want to hear a booming, audible voice. We want an angelic visitation or an open vision. Can God do those things? You better believe He can! However, if you limit Him to just doing that, you will miss His sweet, still, soft voice.

There's a wonderful illustration of this in 1 Kings 19. Elijah had just finished defeating the false prophets of Baal on Mount Carmel and had gone into the wilderness. He was visited by the angel of the Lord, who told Elijah to go up to Mount Horeb, where the Lord would speak to him. He went to Mount Horeb, which is Mount Sinai, where Moses received the Ten Commandments. Then the Lord said:

> "Go out, and stand on the mountain before the LORD." And behold, the LORD passed by, and a great and strong wind tore into the mountains and broke the rocks in pieces before the LORD, but the LORD was not in the wind; and after the wind an earthquake, but the LORD

> was not in the earthquake; and after the earth-
> quake a fire, but the LORD was not in the fire;
> and after the fire a still small voice.
>
> —1 KINGS 19:11–12

This is fascinating because historically, Mount Sinai was known for fire, earthquakes, and rumbling winds. Yet on this occasion the Lord wasn't in any of those things. Had Elijah been fixated on the fire, the wind, or the earthquake, he never would have heard God's voice. But because he recognized that the Lord wasn't in any of the wonders, he was able to hear His still, small voice:

> So it was, when Elijah heard it, that he wrapped
> his face in his mantle and went out and stood
> in the entrance of the cave. Suddenly a voice
> came to him, and said, "What are you doing
> here, Elijah?"
>
> —1 KINGS 19:13

Elijah wrapped his mantle over his head as a sign of reverence and bowed down; then he heard the Lord. Elijah didn't mystify the experience, and he discerned the voice of the Lord.

Don't just look at the wonder. Don't just look at the fire, the earthquake, or the wind. Recognize the Spirit. Elijah was able to recognize the Spirit because he was a man of prayer. Because he spent time with the Lord in prayer, he knew how to recognize and reverence the Lord's voice when he heard it—even when it was only a whisper.

There may be times when you'll be tempted to beg and scream and yell at God so that He speaks to you in some powerful, dramatic way. But if you don't have discernment, you'll miss the whisper. Don't look for the mystifying; seek the Lord.

Having a strong flesh and a weak spirit

The second hang-up when seeking to hear God is equally common—that the flesh is too active and the spirit is too weak. Often our default is to constantly feed the flesh, to constantly feed the distraction. We feed all the noise, and then we wonder why our spirits are atrophied and we're spiritually weak. It's because we don't spend time getting to know God. If you don't position yourself to hear the Lord in prayer and in Scripture, the flesh will be too loud and you won't be able to hear the still, small voice of God. You won't sense the tuning of the Spirit.

This is why you must learn to rest. The Lord will speak to you in His timing, not yours. Many times He speaks to us while we're on the journey. Elijah had to walk from where he was to Mount Horeb and stand before the Lord on that holy mountain. God may take you on a similar journey. God's job is to do the speaking; our job is simply to do the walking. Often God will speak to us along the way.

We may say, "God, I'm not hearing from You." But

if we look back, we will see God's hand, leading and guiding us the entire time. Many times you don't need to hear the voice; you need to be obedient and allow the Lord to stretch you so you'll have the capacity to receive more of Him. Don't get fixated on trying to hear a word—be with the Word.

Needing to see to believe

God is most pleased with your faith, and faith does not require sight. We live by faith, not by external circumstances. We live by faith and not by what we see on the outside. Once we have faith, we see because faith sees. Faith has vision. Even when you don't hear God's voice, you can know you are pleasing God in faith.

The world says, "I have to see it to believe it." Jesus says, "You need to believe to see. You need to believe to hear." Do not base your relationship on whether you feel as if you are hearing or seeing something from God. Rather, secure your footing on the finished work of Christ.

Sometimes we think God is not speaking, or we believe we need to feel something to know He's near. No! The people of God walk by faith. If we try to go through the door of feeling, we will just end up frustrated. But if we go through the door of faith, we will see what God wants to reveal. It is faith that pleases God, and when your heart is in a posture of faith, it is easy to hear from the Spirit.

DON'T GET FIXATED ON TRYING TO HEAR A WORD— BE WITH THE WORD.

Now that you know what not to do, how should you respond when you feel as though you're not hearing from God?

Learn to hide the Word of God in your heart. When you feel as if you're not hearing from God, be like Mary, the mother of Jesus, who "kept all these things in her heart" (Luke 2:19, NLT). As the Word made flesh grew in her womb, Mary tucked all that the angel had spoken into the depths of her being. That's what we must do, especially when God doesn't seem to be speaking the way we want Him to. We must learn to hide His Word in our hearts.

Obey what you heard last. Many times God is like a GPS. When you use a navigational system, it may say, "In two miles turn left." Then it will say nothing else until you pass that second mile. Only then will you hear the voice say, "In five hundred feet turn right." God's "positioning system" is very similar to that. The Lord will speak to you once and will confirm and speak again if needed, but often you must obey what He said at first before you'll hear something else.

FAITH HAS VISION.

If you were using a GPS and it directed you to continue on your route for forty-five miles, you wouldn't give up on it at mile 10. That wouldn't make sense, would it? There are many things like that in our lives. We get frustrated on our journeys and stop listening to God. There will be times of transition and change. When they come, remember to obey what you heard last.

Time in prayer is never wasted time. Time in the Scriptures is never wasted time. The more time you spend with the Lord, the more sensitive to His voice you will become.

Consider this: If I were to tell a baby to sit down, listen, and do what he is told, that baby would just stare at me because he wouldn't be able to comprehend what I had just said. He'd still be a baby. But if I told a five-year-old to sit down, he could do that because he would be more mature.

Growth will cause you to hear God. An infant can't fully comprehend what an adult is saying. The baby needs to grow and become mature in order to hear and obey. Every time you're in prayer and the Word, you are growing in your capacity to receive from God. So don't worry about the mechanics of how God speaks. Focus on growing. Grow in His presence. Grow in His Word. Grow in fellowship with Him, and you will know His voice.

Let's pray:

> *Heavenly Father, I thank You for the gift of salvation and the gift of the Holy Spirit inside us. We thank You for Your Word. Your Word is the primary way in which we can be in tune to hear from You. Help us grow in Your Word and in prayer. Sensitize our hearts in stillness to discern when You're speaking.*
>
> *We love You, Lord. We honor You. Give us eyes to see, ears to hear, and a heart that knows You. As we are renewed day by day in our communion with You, help us understand, Lord, that our call as believers is to minister to You as Your holy priesthood. We are a royal nation of kings and priests unto our God. Lord, teach us to be intimate with You, sharing in the thoughts and feelings of Your heart through the Word and prayer. Lord, reveal to us Your love and grace, and help us grow. In Jesus' name, amen.*

POINTS TO PONDER

- God will freely reveal the deep things of His Spirit to my spirit.

- God resists pride but gives grace to the humble.

- Being attentive in prayer and worshipping God tune me in to receive from His Spirit.

- God draws near to me as I draw near to Him.

Chapter 6

THE SIXTH SECRET: RECOVERING THE MIND OF CHRIST

THERE WAS ONCE a little lion cub that was raised by a bunch of chickens. Because the lion cub was raised by chickens, he began to believe that he was one of the little chicks, so the lion started pecking and clucking like one of them. As the lion grew up, he knew something was missing. He was constantly ridiculed for his lack of feathers and his strange appearance according to the chickens, and he felt he was never good enough to be part of his own community.

Then one day when he was by himself, he looked into a pond. As the waters became still, to his astonishment, he saw his reflection quite clearly. He saw that he did not look like the others and realized why he didn't fit in. He went off to find others who looked like him, and as he raced away, his lion senses kicked in. He found other lions and recovered his true identity. He realized he was a mighty lion. There was nothing wrong with him; he had simply believed the wrong voices and tried to adapt to the wrong circumstances.

In the same way, we must realize that within us is the Lion of the tribe of Judah. For far too long we have received lies, thoughts, and circumstances that projected a reality that is not based on the gospel. We do not have a mind that is merely from this world; we have the mind of Christ.

CR

There are few concepts more electrifying or transformative than Paul's teaching on the mind of Christ. To grasp the revolutionary nature of it, consider 1 Corinthians 2:14–16 (AMPC):

> But the natural, nonspiritual man does not accept or welcome or admit into his heart the gifts and teachings and revelations of the Spirit of God, for they are folly (meaningless nonsense) to him; and he is incapable of knowing them [of progressively recognizing, understanding, and becoming better acquainted with them] because they are spiritually discerned and estimated and appreciated. But the spiritual man tries all things [he examines, investigates, inquires into, questions, and discerns all things], yet is himself to be put on trial and judged by no one [he can read the

meaning of everything, but no one can properly discern or appraise or get an insight into
him]. For who has known or understood the
mind (the counsels and purposes) of the Lord
so as to guide and instruct Him and give Him
knowledge?

But what does he say next? "But we have the
mind of Christ" (1 Cor. 2:16).

We need to believe what the Bible says and harmonize ourselves with the Word. In other words, we
must agree with what God is saying. You might say,
"I don't feel as though I have the mind of Christ."
Having the mind of Christ is not about feelings. It's
about believing. The believer is led by *believing*, not
by feeling.

The simple truth is that "we have the mind
of Christ," as Paul says in verse 16, "and do hold
the thoughts (feelings and purposes) of His heart"
(AMPC). We often think renewing our minds is just
a matter of reprogramming them in a natural way or
following self-help principles. We think it's all about
willpower—that if we confess something enough,
we'll eventually believe it. When you try to change
your mindset in your own strength, you eventually
will return to your old way of thinking because you
are not renewing your mind. Renewing your mind
is not disciplining your thoughts; it's nothing less
than recovering the mind of Christ—His perception,

His outlook, His view of things. That is what is made available to us.

In Romans 12:2, Paul tells us to be transformed by the renewing of our minds that we "may prove what is that good and acceptable and perfect will of God." If we don't renew our minds, we will adopt thinking that is contrary to God's Word and will. We'll begin to see things through natural perspectives. The natural man uses his sense and reason to make decisions, but the spiritual man has the mind of Christ. This is why we must recover His mind daily.

REVELATION UNVEILED

What does it mean to have the mind of Christ or to be renewed in the spirit of your mind? As we saw in previous chapters, the only one who truly knows our thoughts is the spirit within us. It's the same with God. You cannot know the thoughts of God except by His Spirit. (See 1 Corinthians 2:10–11.)

Paul goes further in 1 Corinthians 2:12, saying, "We have not received the spirit [that belongs to] the world, but the [Holy] Spirit Who is from God, [given to us] that we might realize and comprehend and appreciate the gifts [of divine favor and blessing so freely and lavishly] bestowed on us by God" (AMPC). I've said this before, but it bears repeating: Because the Spirit of God is within you, you are able to comprehend His thoughts and the deep things of the Lord. That is what it means to have the mind of Christ. Christ's thoughts are known only by His Spirit within Him. Now that His Spirit is in you, you have access to His mind. That is oneness.

I've been married for ten years and have known my wife for twelve. We're at a point in our relationship where we can have a full conversation simply by giving each other looks. I know what she's thinking and feeling based on her expressions. How? Because I've had fellowship with her. I am one with her in marriage, and I've known her for many years.

We're called to even deeper fellowship with God. It's not two bodies becoming one flesh as it is in marriage. It is the Spirit of God in your spirit—you being joined to His Spirit, and His thoughts becoming yours.

Paul wrote in 1 Corinthians 2:13, "And we are setting these truths forth in words not taught by human wisdom but taught by the [Holy] Spirit, combining and interpreting spiritual truths with spiritual language [to those who possess the Holy Spirit]" (AMPC). The Holy Spirit comes to be our teacher. He takes the truth of God's Word, compares it with other truth in Scripture, and then reveals the truth to us, giving us understanding. In other words, He breathes revelation into the Scripture.

There is no such thing as a new revelation. All revelation is an unveiling of the truth of God's

Word. The problem with the Pharisees is that they knew the written Word but missed the Word made flesh because they had no revelation. Revelation is not filling your head with knowledge that puffs up—it is allowing the Holy Spirit to become your teacher and unveil truths in Scripture that you've never understood. It was the Holy Spirit who wrote the Scriptures. It was the Holy Spirit who inspired the Word of God, and it takes the Holy Spirit to interpret it.

The Greek word translated "revelation" is *apokalypsis*. It's where we get the word *apocalypse*. That is why the Book of Apocalypse is called the Book of Revelation—because apocalypse means revealing.[1]

It's one thing to say, "I have the mind of Christ." It's another to have the revelation of that. If you knew that, you would see how overwhelmingly powerful that truth is and it would change your whole life.

During altar calls a well-known evangelist friend of mine used to say, "Do you know what separates us from heaven and hell? Thirteen inches." When I first heard him say that, I thought, "What is he talking about? Thirteen inches?" But he went on to explain that there are thirteen inches between the mind and the heart. His point was that many people give Jesus their mental assent. They know about Him, but they don't have a revelation of who He is.

It's not enough just to fill your head with Bible facts. You must know the Word. You must know the context of the Scriptures. That is what God wants for you. He wants to unveil His Word so it becomes personal and comes alive to you. He wants it to truly become spiritual manna—food for your spirit. When that happens, the Word will begin to renew, recover, and revive you so your thoughts are no longer natural but reflect the mind and thoughts of Christ.

You can't know the Lord through natural means. As I've said before, the natural man is ruled by his reason and senses. He does not welcome into his heart the gifts and revelations of the Spirit of God because they are complete nonsense to him. The Bible says he is incapable of knowing them. The natural man can't comprehend the mind of Christ because it is discerned spiritually. "But the spiritual man," Paul writes, "tries all things [he examines, investigates, inquires into, questions, and discerns all things]" (1 Cor. 2:15, AMPC). Discernment is not suspicion. True discernment is not just seeing what's right and wrong. It's seeing what is God and what is flesh. It's seeing by the Spirit what is true and what is false.

Paul continues in 1 Corinthians 2:16: "For who has known or understood the mind (the counsels and purposes) of the Lord so as to guide and instruct Him and give Him knowledge? But we have the mind of Christ (the Messiah) and do hold the thoughts (feelings and purposes) of His heart" (AMPC). Why? Because we have His Spirit.

As a man "thinks in his heart, so is he" (Prov. 23:7). So we need to ask ourselves, "What am I minding?" The antithesis of the renewing of your mind is the reviving of your flesh. If you mind the flesh, the flesh is going to be renewed and produce corruption. But if you mind the things of the Spirit, you will have not only His mind but also life and peace. Are you minding the appetites of your flesh? Do you wallow in self-condemnation or a works-based religiosity? Are you minding legalism and fear? Be careful not to think, "That's just how I am." Feeding your mind with wrong perceptions of God and what He's like will keep you from fully experiencing His presence.

A PRACTICAL GUIDE TO RENEWING YOUR MIND

But how do we recover the mind of Christ in our lives? Romans 8:5 says, "For those who are according to the flesh and are controlled by its unholy desires set their minds on and pursue those things which gratify the flesh" (AMPC). Why do people gratify the flesh? Because they set their minds on and pursue fleshly things. "But," the verse continues, "those who are according to the Spirit and are controlled by the desires of the Spirit set their minds on and seek those things which gratify the [Holy] Spirit." What you're pursuing is what you're minding.

What are you pursuing in your thought life? Is it the impulses and the gratifications of your flesh? Is it a wrong belief about who you are and how God sees you? Is it legalism or religious thinking? "Seek those things which gratify the [Holy] Spirit" (Rom. 8:5, AMPC). What gratifies the Holy Spirit? Prayer, worship, reading the Word, engaging in relationship with God, and allowing the Holy Spirit to help you say no to this world—all these things do. When you yield to Him, you will find yourself seeking and pursuing the things that gratify the Spirit.

The renewing of your mind, then, is the minding of the Spirit. Mind the things of God. Have you ever heard the expression "Mind your own business"? Well, I challenge you to mind the business of the Spirit. What is His business? It is His thoughts that are penned in the Word of God. I urge you to allow yourself to mind Him. Mind the Holy Spirit in prayer. Mind Him in Scripture reading. Mind Him throughout your day, and you will see life and peace. You see, it's by receiving the promises in God's Word that we partake of His divine nature. You are a child of God. You have the mind of Christ. You have the thoughts and feelings of His heart. You can walk in this reality if you will receive what He is saying.

Second Peter 1:3 says, "For His divine power has bestowed upon us all things that [are requisite and suited] to life and godliness" (AMPC). How is this life and godliness received? The answer is in the same verse: "through the [full, personal] knowledge of Him Who called us by and to His own glory and excellence (virtue)" (2 Pet. 1:3, AMPC).

All things related to life and godliness are given through an avenue. The knowledge of God is not just intellect or reason. It is knowing the Lord.

Peter wrote, "Grace and peace be multiplied to you in the knowledge of God and of Jesus our Lord, as His divine power has given to us all things that pertain to life and godliness, through the knowledge of Him" (2 Pet. 1:2–3). The word translated as "knowledge" in this verse is the Greek term *epignōsis*. It refers to "precise and correct knowledge"[2] and the "knowledge of a particular point," directed toward a specific object. It is perception, recognition, discernment, and intuition.[3]

The knowledge of God is knowledge directed toward Him. It is the perception of God, the discernment of God, the recognition of God, and the intuition of God. To have the knowledge of God is to perceive, discern, recognize, and have intuitive acquaintance with Him. That comes only by knowing the Lord through His Word and Spirit. In other words, it comes only through relationship.

In the phrasing of Peter:

> His divine power has given to us all things
> that pertain to life and godliness, through
> the knowledge of Him who called us by glory
> and virtue, by which have been given to us
> exceedingly great and precious promises, that
> through these you may be partakers of the
> divine nature, having escaped the corruption
> that is in the world through lust.
>
> —2 PETER 1:3-4

Do you want to escape corruption and get away from carnal thinking? You must receive the great and precious promises given to us through the Word of God. This is how you become partakers of the divine nature. By minding God's Word and Spirit, you partake of this reality, and you see Him rightly.

We become what we behold. This is the renewing of the mind.

THE FEAR OF GOD

The fear of God is a crucial component in the renewal of our minds. This topic is so often misunderstood. I'm not talking about an earthly fear. This is not about being scared of God, as if He's going to hit you or something. The fear of God is a response of holy reverence. It is being so awed by His love and beauty that the thought of displeasing Him brings sorrow to your heart.

This is why the renewal of our minds is so deeply

connected to a renewal of our hearts. Our minds are not just being renewed intellectually; we are in a process of becoming spiritually sensitive to the things that move God's heart. When we fear the Lord, not only do we think in alignment with God's thoughts for us, but we are sensitive to God's emotions and feel what He feels. Our minds are renewed, yes, but ultimately it is our hearts that are made soft.

WE BECOME WHAT WE BEHOLD. THIS IS THE RENEWING OF THE MIND.

You have been given the priceless gift of knowing God. You have been given the overwhelming treasure of receiving the mind of Christ. When you keep going before Him every day, saying, "I offer my life to You," that is worship. Slowly but surely as you continue to offer yourself as a living sacrifice to Him, you will begin to recover the mind of Christ in your life. You will begin to experience oneness with Him. His thoughts will become your thoughts and His feelings your feelings. *That* is the renewing of your mind!

Join me in praying that the Lord would give us the mind of Christ.

Heavenly Father, thank You for the great privilege of experiencing Your very presence. Lord, I ask You in the mighty name of Jesus to flood us with the thoughts of Christ and unveil the mind of Jesus within us. Thank You, Lord, for renewing, transforming, and empowering our minds, thoughts, and feelings. Father, expose every lie from the enemy, every lie from the flesh, and every lie from life circumstances—direct them to the truth of who You are. May we see who we are in You! I thank You for giving us the mind of Christ and for making us one with You. In Jesus' mighty name, amen!

POINTS TO PONDER

- I have the mind of Christ through the Holy Spirit.

- God is the One who renews my mind and brings me from one degree of glory to the next.

- God wants to reveal the mind of Christ to me through His Word and Spirit.

- Christ's thoughts will become my thoughts when I surrender to Him and pursue things that gratify the Spirit.

Chapter 7

THE SEVENTH SECRET: CHRIST IN YOU

ONCE THERE WAS a man who was invited to a treasure hunt by a teacher. His teacher gave him a map to this treasure as well as a special briefcase he was to keep with him at all times. The treasure hunter was told that the key to the briefcase was buried at the treasure site.

The treasure hunter spent months locating the treasure site. At last, he found it—and the key! He thought he would find within the briefcase special tools to dig up this treasure. But to his amazement, when he put the key into the special briefcase, he didn't find tools to dig up the treasure—he found the treasure itself! The treasure had been with him the entire time, but the valuables had been completely hidden from him.

Something glorious was kept hidden for ages and generations that has now been revealed to us, the children of God. We find it in Colossians 1:19: "For it pleased the Father that in Him all the fullness should dwell." What does that mean? Who is "Him"? Jesus—in Jesus all the fullness should dwell. The fullness of what? The fullness of *all* things. The fullness of God. The fullness of the Father, the Spirit, and the Son.

Then we read in Colossians 1:20, "And by Him to reconcile all things to Himself, by Him, whether things on earth or things in heaven, having made peace through the blood of His cross." The Jesus we serve, the Jesus preached in the gospel, is not just some philosopher or religious teacher. The fullness of *all* things resides in Jesus. He is higher than all things. He is supreme above everything that was, is, and will be. Jesus is the Alpha and Omega—the First and the Last. He's the Beginning and the End. He's the King of kings and Lord of lords. He is the Prince of Peace. He is the way. He is the truth. He is the life. He is the highest being that could ever exist. All things were created by Him and through Him.

Everything that exists is held together by the whim of His will. That is Jesus. That is our King. All the fullness of the Godhead dwells in Him, and by Him *all things* are reconciled to Himself. What are those things? They are "things on earth, things in heaven, having made peace through the blood of His cross" (Col. 1:20).

You know what's amazing? As John 3:16 tells us, "For God so loved the world that He gave His only begotten Son, that whoever believes in Him should not perish but have everlasting life." Because this verse is so familiar, we may miss the scandal and power of these words. I love the word *world* here because in the Greek (*kosmos*) it essentially refers to the created order.[1] Jesus came, became the perfect offering to bring people to Himself, and reconciled not just people but all of creation to Himself. Jesus will make all things new. It's not just "I die and go to heaven." He came so that we might become alive to Him and be reconciled, and so that everything that exists—the universe, the whole created order—will be made right before Him.

Romans 8 says that the whole earth groans with travail for "the manifestation of the sons of God" (vv. 19, 22, KJV). It groans in anticipation of that day when every tear will be wiped away and the old order of things will be no more. (See Revelation 21:4.) In that day, death will no longer exist. There will be a new heaven and a new earth. Jesus is coming not just to save a people but to save all of creation. Again, He will redeem not just some things but *all* things.

Now, what are those things? They are the created things, or things in heaven. The word *heaven* is the created heavens, the expanse. One day they're going to be rolled away like a scroll, but then they will be made new. Paul tells us that the cross of Jesus has already disarmed the principalities and powers. (See

Colossians 2:15.) He explains, "And you, who once were alienated and enemies in your mind by wicked works, yet now He has reconciled in the body of His flesh through death, to present you holy, and blameless, and above reproach in His sight—if indeed you continue in the faith, grounded and steadfast, and are not moved away from the hope of the gospel which you heard, which was preached to every creature under heaven, of which I, Paul, became a minister" (Col. 1:21–23). Then, in Colossians 1:26 he begins to talk about the secret, or "the mystery which has been hidden from ages and from generations, but now has been revealed to His saints."

Allow yourself to sit with that phrase for a moment: "revealed to His saints." That's *you*. That's *me*. We are saints. "Well, I don't feel like a saint," you say. Listen, if you've received Jesus, you have already been translated from the kingdom of darkness into the kingdom of light. Your identity was that of a sinful sinner, and now you are a separated saint.

So we see in Colossians 1:26 that there's a mystery that has been hidden from ages and generations but now has been revealed to His saints (to us!). Colossians 1:27 continues that to the saints "God willed to make known what are the riches of the glory of this mystery among the Gentiles: which is…" Which is…are you ready? The mystery "which is *Christ in you, the hope of glory*" (1 Col. 1:27, emphasis added). *This* is the secret that now has been revealed. *Christ in you*. That is the hope of glory. According to Colossians 1:28, then, "Him we preach, warning every man and teaching every man in all wisdom, that we may present every man perfect in Christ Jesus." This is an ongoing journey and a progressive revelation that has already been established by the authority of God's Word. Do you realize what a great and precious promise that is—that Jesus of Nazareth lives on the inside of you?

We have considered many things here that I hope will be helpful; there are many keys to a life of prayer and surrender. But there is only one "secret" to a life in God—only one secret that changes everything—and that is the revelation of Christ in you. The mystery that all of creation has longed to see, and that angels and prophets and patriarchs have all longed to bear witness to, is the Christ who is at work inside you now. If you are in Christ, there is nothing "out there" that anyone has to sell or give to you that you need. What if the thing you most desperately need is simply to be jolted awake to recognize the true power that already resides inside you?

HE THAT LIVES WITHIN YOU

I'll put it to you this way: What would happen if you received revelation for yourself, and by the Holy Spirit, God made the truth of this word alive to you? What would it change? You would see and conduct yourself with total reverence because Jesus is on the inside of you. This is why many times all throughout Scripture we are commanded to be holy—because the Holy One dwells on the inside of us. This is why Paul says, "The body...is not meant for sexual immorality but for the Lord" (1 Cor. 6:13, NIV). Then he says, "Don't you realize that your body is the temple of the Holy Spirit" and the Spirit of almighty God lives on the inside of you? (v. 19, NLT). This is already the reality, but the time has come for you to fully awaken to what already is. Ask the Holy Spirit to make that reality alive on the inside of you.

I liken this reality to a woman who's pregnant. Have you ever experienced or seen this process? It's beautiful because there is a glow about her. People notice, and she takes tremendous care of herself. She prepares for the arrival of that child. She does everything with the mindset that there's a baby in her womb. That baby gives her cravings, and she starts to eat things that she typically doesn't eat. Why? There's a little one growing in her womb, so she takes special care of herself. In the same way, this is how we ought to conduct ourselves. The Holy One is on the inside of us. The Spirit of God is in the deepest parts of our being. If we acknowledge that truth—that Christ is in us—we will devote ourselves to caring for our spiritual well-being and He will give us cravings that align with His Word.

A CLEAN HOUSE FOR FELLOWSHIP

Be still and know that He is God. When our hearts are postured in this way, God begins to accomplish infinitely more than what we can imagine. When we learn to rest in His holy presence and just be with Him, He rearranges the affections, the attentions, and the longings of the heart because we are ministering to the Holy Spirit. As we minister unto Him, He begins to rearrange the furniture in our hearts. So many times our hearts are cluttered, like houses full of junk. But as we wait on the Lord, as we minister to God, and as we learn to worship Him and be with Him, the Holy Spirit begins to clean our houses for fellowship.

We are distracted by so many things in life from the moment we wake up to the time we sleep. So it's always important to understand that the focus of a believer's life is to be with the Lord. His presence is enriching. His presence is satisfying. His presence purifies. His presence enlivens the heart and enlivens the spirit. The Lord deemed His presence very important. In Exodus 33:15–16 Moses cried out in a loud voice, saying, "If your Presence does not go with us.... What else will distinguish [us] from all the other people on the face of the earth?" (NIV). The Lord promised to do this, having said, "My Presence will go with you, and I will give you rest" (Exod. 33:14).

Out of all the nations and all the peoples of the

earth, what distinctly made Israel separate, set apart, was the presence of God in their midst—that presence that brings divine *rest*. The God of glory tabernacled and made His dwelling place with Israel. The glory of God resided in a cloud and dwelled in the tabernacle, the meeting place between Moses and God. The scripture says that God spoke to Moses "face to face, as a man speaks to his friend" (Exod. 33:11). The word *face* there is the Hebrew word *pānîm*. It's "presence."[2] The face of the Lord is the presence of the Lord. If you are not at rest, if you are not at peace in your life, there is literally no solution other than the experience of His presence, of the One who longs to speak to you as a friend, face to face.

OUR LIVING TABERNACLE

To give someone your face is to give them your attention. It is to give them your sight—eyes connecting, hearts connecting. This is what it means to be in fellowship with the presence of God. Not that we're seeking a literal face or a visionary experience of a face, but we're putting our attention on the person of the Lord. Again, what distinguishes us from all the peoples of the earth? It is the presence of God abiding with us, and us abiding with Him.

After the man of God, Moses, died, there was a

transition point where Israel went from a tabernacle to a tent of David. David's political strategy was not his wars, not his armies, and not his excellent military campaign. David's political strategy was the presence of God, and he established the tent of God's presence. When he became king over Israel, there was twenty-four-hour unhindered access to the very presence of God. This was a wonderful type and shadow of Jesus our King, who gave us, the people of God, twenty-four-hour access to the presence of the Lord. The holy prophets declared that the days were coming when the fallen tent of David was going to be restored, and after King David died, his son Solomon began to build a temple. It was a beautiful physical dwelling place wherein the holy of holies—the heavy weight of the presence and power of God—was in the midst of His people.

Whenever Israel went astray, God sent prophets to call them back and tell them to return and repent of their idolatries—to let go of the whoredoms of this world and be betrothed back to the Lord. When they did not listen, the temple was destroyed, the presence of God lifted, and the glory departed. Then we fast-forward to the time when the temple was rebuilt during the days of Hosea, Zerubbabel, and Jeshua, the high priest. We see that the people returned from their Babylonian exile back to Jerusalem, back to Israel. God continued to be with them, but there was four hundred years of silence from Malachi to

Matthew—four hundred years of no prophetic voice, four hundred years of no glory in their midst, and four hundred years of a holy pause. The time span of four hundred years is symbolic because Israel was held captive by Egypt for four hundred years. During those four hundred years they cried out and God sent them Moses.

Skipping ahead from Malachi to Matthew, a new Moses emerges—one who does not turn water into blood but water into wine. He was not just a teacher but the Word made flesh—not just a prophet but a prophecy wrapped in a body: Jesus of Nazareth. In the language of John's Gospel, "In the beginning was the Word, and the Word was with God, and the Word was God....And the Word became flesh" (John 1:1, 14). The Word literally tabernacled among humanity. The glory and presence of God was wrapped in a body, and God began to dwell with His people yet again. Jesus, the living tabernacle, is our living tent of meeting, and He begins the promise of the Father: the presence of almighty God, the Holy Spirit.

LIVING WATER

In John 7:38 Jesus says in a loud voice, "He who believes in Me, as the Scripture has said, out of his heart will flow rivers of living water." He signifies the Spirit for those who would receive this tabernacle—the

Lord Jesus, the presence of God in our midst. This living tabernacle takes upon Himself the sin of the world. He takes upon Himself your shame, your guilt, and your condemnation and makes all things new. He takes the old and converts it into the new. He takes you from darkness into light.

The story that began when God spoke creation into existence in Genesis 1 now comes full circle. We see a mystery—a secret that has been hidden from ages and generations but now has been revealed to his saints—which is Christ in you, the hope of glory. Jesus is the living glory of God now residing in the hearts of those who would receive Him. The fellowship that was broken in the Garden of Eden has now been restored. No longer are you just following Jesus from afar. You have Him in you, and you are in Him. This is the great mystery that is revealed to the church, and God wants us to recover that back again.

What would happen if you truly saw yourself as the bearer of Christ? What would happen if you truly saw yourself as a tabernacle of Christ? You would see yourself in a whole different light. You would see yourself according to *His* light. The life and light of men is Christ in you, the hope of glory.

In Him you are finally restored to your original vocation, the thing you were literally born to do. From the beginning we were created to be images of God. Another way of saying this is "reflections."

We are to reflect Christ—the light is not in ourselves. It is all Him. We reflect Him as we receive Him. Now that the mystery has been revealed to us and is in us, we are free to be the people we were always designed to be and to fulfill the purpose God always had for us in the earth.

WHAT WOULD HAPPEN IF YOU TRULY SAW YOURSELF AS THE BEARER OF CHRIST?

He invites you to understand the truth of Christ in you, the revelation that changes everything. Many believers have a very defeated mindset. They have a very low view of themselves. They call it humility when really it is false humility and pride. We must agree with what God's Word says about Him and about us, regardless of how we feel. Our feelings are fickle and fleeting; they come and go. We must stand on the truth of God's Word—Jesus, the Anointed One, resides on the inside of you.

HOLY HABITATION

We are a tent of His very glory. Peter in his closing letter knew that his time was coming to an end. As an old man, he was ready for martyrdom. So in 2 Peter he says, "I am in this tent" (1:13). He calls his body "this tent" and says that he's ready to lay aside his earthly tent (v. 14). You see, this body is just a dwelling place. This is why we must understand that we are called to live a set-apart life. We are called to be separate from sin and perversions and evil. We are His holy habitation. Am I saying that you'll never sin again? No. But 1 John 1:9 says, "If we confess our sins, He is faithful and just to forgive us our sins and to cleanse us from all unrighteousness." Yet He does not want us to live in habitual sin. That is beneath our vocation and beneath our calling—beneath the revelation of who we really are in Him.

We read earlier how Paul had to rebuke the carnal Corinthians for their immorality. They loved Jesus— they were lacking in no spiritual gift. They were anointed. They were gifted. They were speaking in tongues and prophesying. But there was immorality, carnality, divisions, and contentions in their midst. The corrective measure brought by the apostle Paul was: "Don't you realize who you are? Don't you realize that your body is the temple of the Holy Spirit? Don't you realize that Christ is in you?" Ask the Holy Spirit to unveil this reality in your life. As He does this, you will carry yourself in a whole different light. You will actually honor and reverence yourself and others. You'll learn to love yourself and love others because you are a vessel that contains the very glory of the Lord.

Paul describes himself as a broken vessel—an

earthen vessel that contains the power and glory of God—so that it's clear that this glory is not of us (2 Cor. 4:7). Your earthly body is just the shell. But because of Christ in you, you become a vessel of honor and a vessel of purity—a vessel of His magnificence. When you see that reality, you will have a whole different relationship with sin. You will carry yourself with the dignity that comes from Him. You will see yourself as the house of God, a house of glory.

Think about that. Whenever you have an offense—because offenses will come—whenever there's discord, disagreement, disunity, and disharmony with other brothers and sisters in the Lord, before you're quick to snap back and see them as your enemy, remember that they too are a house of glory. They too have Christ in them.

This is why we have to say, "Greater is he that is in [me], than he that is in the world" (1 John 4:4, KJV). When the temptations of the world overwhelm you, when the distractions of this age come against you, and when all these things begin to billow through, remind yourself of this reality: "Greater is he that is in you, than he that is in the world." He lives in you. This is why when you wake up in the morning, you feel that unction to spend time with Him. This is why during certain moments you feel the need to be alone with Him. This is why when the temptations of sin come, there's a prodding on the inside of you that says, "Don't do that; that grieves Me." Why? Because He's *in* you.

I am very aware that no amount of information can change your life—only revelation. So I want to draw this chapter to a close not with more concepts but a prayer that I hope will open you up to the mystery of the ages. He sees you, He knows you, and He is so much more eager than you could imagine to be seen and known!

If you do not know Christ, I invite you to turn away from darkness, from sin, and turn to Christ. Confess that you're in need of Him, and receive Him using the following prayer as a guide:

> *Lord, I know that I'm in sin. I know I'm a sinner. I need forgiveness. I receive the free gift of eternal life, Your Son. I repent of my sin, and I make You Lord and Savior of my life. Jesus, I believe You died on the cross for me. I believe You were raised from the dead. I receive You into my life. I make You my Lord, my Savior. I give You my whole being. Amen.*

That's the truth of the gospel. If you prayed that for the first time, welcome to the family of God. The mystery beneath all other mysteries now surges through you—Christ in you, the hope of glory!

POINTS TO PONDER

- I am a dwelling place for the presence, glory, and power of God.

- I must turn my eyes toward Jesus and away from my sins.

- I am made in the image of God.

- I have been invited to experience God's glory.

Chapter 8

THE EIGHTH SECRET: THE SONSHIP OF THE SPIRIT

THERE IS A magnificent section in Romans 8 where Paul describes the sons of God. As it builds, pay attention to how he narrates how the children of God live—those who have received sonship through the Spirit. Who are the sons of God?

> Therefore, brethren, we are debtors—not to the flesh, to live according to the flesh. For if you live according to the flesh you will die; but if by the Spirit you put to death the deeds of the body, you will live.
>
> —ROMANS 8:12–13

If you live according to the dictates, or impulses, of the sinful nature, you will die. The sinful nature produces corruption, "for the wages of sin is death" (Rom. 6:23).

The invitation is not for us to overcome sin through

our own strength but to live "by the Spirit." Now, many believers will try to live right by their own willpower or in accordance with their own fleshly mindset. We are not called to put to death the deeds of the body by our own might. This is why we fall—because we take our eyes off Jesus. Remember the story of Peter walking on water? He could not walk above the water on his own. It was impossible. But in the presence of Jesus, Peter did the impossible because the presence of Jesus sustained him. In the same way, we as believers cannot live a holy life apart from the presence of Christ. Being in the presence of Jesus is being in the presence of the Spirit. And by the Spirit we do the impossible—we put to death the deeds of the sinful nature.

You cannot overcome by yourself; it is only by the Spirit. Isn't that freeing? You're not bound to live a life of cycles of condemnation. God wants you to walk in and by the Spirit. Again, many times we look at the spectacular and miss the supernatural. We look at the spectacular miracles and encounters—and there's nothing wrong with that—but it is equally supernatural to put to death the deeds of the body by the Holy Spirit. If by the Spirit you put to death the deeds of the body, you will live. It is the grace of God—it is all Him.

Our lives must be a progression of surrendering and yielding to the Spirit. Romans 8:14 says, "For as many as are led by the Spirit of God, these are the sons of God." Again, who are the sons of God? You and I are sons of God. There is only one unique begotten Son of God—that is Jesus of Nazareth. And yet to those who have received Him, the Scripture tells us, "He gave the right to become children of God" (John 1:12).

YOU CANNOT OVERCOME BY YOURSELF; IT IS ONLY BY THE SPIRIT.

The word *begotten* in the Bible means unique.[1] It reminds me of the story of Abraham. The Bible says Abraham had two sons: a son from the flesh, which was Ishmael, and a son of promise, which was Isaac. Both were his natural children, but only one of them was the unique son of promise—a beautiful type and shadow of the Messiah. God tells Abraham, "Take your son, your only son, and take him to Mount Moriah and sacrifice him to Me" (Gen. 22:2, paraphrased). Some Torah commentators say that Isaac was in his thirties when he willingly went up with his father to offer the sacrifice. This is a dazzling image of the way Jesus, at thirty-three years old, would willingly sacrifice His own life.[2]

While Jesus is unique as the only begotten Son of God, keep in mind that the One who died on the cross also told us that we must take up our cross and follow Him. (See Matthew 16:24.) We are not to be led around by our fleshly desires, by our impulses, or by our physical senses.

The word *led* is another word for "to bring."[3] Another way of saying this could be "to yield." Those who are led are *submitted*; they are yielded.

The reason that this is not self-help, but not some dour self-sacrifice either, where we have to live anxious and with clenched teeth all the time, is because of Romans 8:15: "For you did not receive the spirit of bondage again to fear, but you received the Spirit of adoption by whom we cry out, 'Abba, Father.'" Everything changes when you realize your reality is now grounded entirely in this relationship.

This is also a wonderful key to prayer. Enter into prayer knowing that God is your Father and you are His son or daughter. In the Sermon on the Mount, Jesus repeatedly refers to God as Father—and it's the same concept. Many times we go to Him with an orphan mentality. We need to realize that when we approach His presence, while we are in the presence of a great and mighty King, He also happens to be our heavenly Father. You have been adopted into the royal family of God through the precious blood of Jesus. "We cry out, 'Abba, Father.'" It's a beautiful, childlike expression, like saying "Papa" or "Dad." It's a family term.

When I was about eighteen years old and getting

my driver's license, I remember seeing a Jewish man walk into the office with a little girl behind him. She was pulling his coat and saying, "Abba, Abba, Abba!" She was his little daughter. That's the terminology that Paul is giving us here. We've been adopted into the royal family of God. Romans 8:16 continues, "The Spirit Himself bears witness with our spirit that we are children of God." When you've received the Lord, deep down you *know* you belong to Him. You may not feel this all the time, but this is a knowing that's deeper than your feelings. *The Spirit* bears witness with our spirits, and there is a deep, inward knowing.

AN ENSLAVED MINDSET

You must also understand that you're a son or you're a daughter. He's your Father. You must approach Him as your heavenly Father. You must see Him as your Abba. Do not, even for a moment, doubt that. Many times we approach Him incorrectly. What did the disciples say to Jesus? "Teach us to pray," and He said, "When you pray, say: Our Father..." (Luke 11:1–2). The first thing Jesus teaches the disciples, in the area of prayer, is to recognize God as their Father. That must be the key ingredient. That's how to see correctly. Don't see things in accordance with the way you have been raised or where you came from. See yourself in accordance with how God sees you in His Word. When you do, everything changes. Now you're not a begging slave; you're a victorious son, a victorious daughter.

Many believers have a slavery mindset—they've been enslaved by the lusts of the flesh and the sins of this world. When they received Him, they received Him as Savior but still had the mind of Egypt. They're like the children of Israel: Moses comes in, he delivers them, they go into the wilderness—and they want to go back to Egypt! Even though Moses takes them out of Egypt, Egypt is still in them. That whole generation has to die off for the next generation to come into the new promise.

NEW WINE

No one takes old wineskins and puts new wine in them, Jesus said, lest they burst. New wine goes into new wineskins. (See Luke 5:37–39.) That's why you might be about to burst. You're receiving the truth of God's Word, you're seeing the wine of the gospel, but your container, your mindset, is unrenewed. It's like an old wineskin. They're incompatible with each other. You've got to adopt the new mindset, the new perspective that the gospel offers you. Notice it's the new covenant. All things are new. Another way of saying this is it is a covenant of newness. In His presence He's ever new. His mercies are new. Everything is new. Out with the old, in with the new. Out with your old mindset. Out with your old mentality.

You want to experience the new wine? The Pharisees could not receive what Jesus was saying or doing because He spoke from a new place. The Pharisees were still caught up in the old wineskin. Many believers love Jesus, but they have an old-wineskin perception. Their thought life is all based on their past. You cannot plow the field and look behind you. Jesus tells us that a disciple must plow forward and not look back. He that does look back is not fit to enter the kingdom. (See Luke 9:62.) What does this have to do with anything? It has to do with everything. Don't come to Jesus with your old perspectives. Don't come to Him with the old man. Come to Him as the renewed man—as a son or daughter of God.

IN HIS PRESENCE, HE'S EVER NEW. HIS MERCIES ARE NEW.

Romans 8:31 says, "What then shall we say to these things? If God is for us, who can be against us?" The reality is that God *is* for you. If you belong to Jesus, stop thinking that He's against you. That's an old-wineskin mentality. Scripture tells us very clearly that if any man is in Christ, he's a new creation altogether (2 Cor. 5:17). The old has passed away. The new has come. "He who did not spare His own Son, but delivered Him up for us all, how shall He not with Him also freely give us all things?" (Rom. 8:32). The hardest thing was sending Jesus. The next six verses make one of the most breathtaking passages in all of the New Testament:

> Who shall bring a charge against God's elect? It is God who justifies. Who is he who condemns? It is Christ who died, and furthermore is also risen, who is even at the right hand of God, who also makes intercession for us. Who shall separate us from the love of Christ? Shall tribulation, or distress, or persecution, or famine, or nakedness, or peril, or sword? As it is written: "For Your sake we are killed all day long; we are accounted as sheep for the slaughter." Yet in all these things we are more than conquerors through Him who loved us.
>
> —ROMANS 8:33–37

You are more than a conqueror through Him who loved you. Then Paul goes on to say,

> For I am persuaded that neither death nor life, nor angels nor principalities nor powers, nor things present nor things to come, nor height nor depth, nor any other created thing, shall be able to separate us from the love of God which is in Christ Jesus our Lord.
>
> —ROMANS 8:38–39

Why can we be convinced that absolutely nothing in heaven or on earth or below the earth, no force or power, can separate us from His love? Because of the fierce power of this relationship already established in Christ. Because He is our Father and we've been adopted into His family. Stop magnifying principalities and angels and powers or things to come. Magnify the power of His great love.

Take that to prayer when you approach the Lord. Don't look at yourself as a begging peasant. Don't have a slave mentality where you're just groveling on the floor, waiting for God to give you a bone. You're His child. You're a son. You're a daughter. You are treasured. You are meant to be led by Him—led by His Spirit and His Word. No matter what comes your way, you've got to have that perspective. It will change the way you pray. I pray you're able to take Romans 8, digest it, chew on it, consume it, and then pray it. Make it your own. Hide the Word in your heart.

I pray that you would approach Him in prayer as a son or daughter to your Abba. I pray that you would let go of your old wineskin and put on the new man who is re-created in Christ Jesus—the new wineskin able to comprehend the new wine. I pray that your spirit is stirred, encouraged, refreshed, and edified. I pray that you would be so in tune with the Father in your identity as His son or daughter that you go and turn the world upside down for His kingdom and for His glory.

Let's pray:

> *Heavenly Father, I ask You right now in the mighty name of Jesus Christ to unveil to us our Sonship and reveal to us who we are— sons and daughters of the Most High God. I ask You now by the power of Your Holy Spirit to reveal to us that what You have given us causes us to grow in maturity. It causes us to see You rightly, through the lens of Your Word and the wind of Your Spirit. We ask You, Lord God, to illuminate who we truly are in You. In Jesus Christ's name I pray, amen.*

POINTS TO PONDER

- I must let go of old mindsets to receive the fresh oil of the Holy Spirit.

- God doesn't want to bring me back to the way things were; He wants to bring me into greater glory.

- I am called to behold God's glory.

- I am a son or daughter of God, and He is my Father.

Conclusion

PRAY TO SEE

I N 2011 I had the opportunity to visit Fond Parisien, one of the poorest regions in all of Haiti and possibly the world. I saw poverty in that area that would break even the toughest hearts. At one local orphanage, the poverty was so intense the children didn't even have adequate clothing. During that visit I was ambushed by little children wanting to greet me. I took out my small camera and began taking pictures and videos of the kids as they clapped and sang.

One kid was especially curious about my camera. As I showed him how it worked, he just stared at himself on the screen. It was as if he had never really seen himself. To my surprise and disbelief, he hadn't! Many of the kids were mesmerized by their own image. It was as if they were responding to a magic trick or something. They may have seen their reflection in a pond, a stream, or perhaps a metal pot but never in an actual mirror.

When we think of a mirror, we think of "a polished

or smooth surface (as of glass) that forms images by reflection" or "something that gives a true representation."[1] But in biblical times mirrors weren't perfectly clear. Back then mirrors were often made of polished brass or copper, so they created dim reflections, and you had to look intently, often with a light, to see yourself. Knowing this adds a great deal of context to Paul's words to the church in Corinth:

> When I was a child, I spoke as a child, I understood as a child, I thought as a child; but when I became a man, I put away childish things. *For now we see in a mirror, dimly, but then face to face.* Now I know in part, but then I shall know just as I also am known.
> —1 CORINTHIANS 13:11–12,
> EMPHASIS ADDED

On this side of heaven, we are going to see and understand things dimly, but a time is coming when we will see Christ face to face in all His glory and radiance.

My favorite scripture of all time is 2 Corinthians 3:18:

> But we all, with unveiled face, beholding as in a mirror the glory of the Lord, are being transformed into the same image from glory to glory, just as by the Spirit of the Lord.

When we turn to Christ, the veil of spiritual blindness is removed. And we with unveiled faces behold as in a mirror the glory of the Lord and are transformed into the likeness and image of the One we behold—Christ. You become what you behold. But you must understand that just like the ancient Corinthians looking in those primitive mirrors, you need to look purposefully and with the light of God's Word. Right now you are not meant to see God's fullness with perfect clarity. This transformation is progressive; you go from one degree of glory to the next. Your responsibility is to behold.

You are not going to see everything up front. You will see glimpse by glimpse.

Oftentimes believers get frustrated because they want to see the Lord through the lens of their own feelings, past experiences, or preconceived thoughts about what God is like. But there is only one real way to look intently at Him, and it is through the lens of Scripture.

You can see God only in the mirror of His Word. As you reflect on that mirror by ingesting His Word, and allowing Him to reveal it to you, you will see Him with greater accuracy and clarity, and you will be changed into what you behold. Be intentional in looking, and as you keep looking unto Christ through the Word, you will see more of Him from glory to glory!

You were meant to bear the image of God and

reflect His glory on this earth. But in order to properly reflect Him, you must reflect on His Word. With each small glimpse into His person through His Word, you will reflect more of Him.

Seeing God's glory is not a physical seeing; it is a spiritual perceiving of His presence and goodness. It is being aware of God's glory in your life. It is not receiving a vision or image of His face, though visions can be part of a believer's life. Rather, it is reflecting upon Him and lifting your heart to Him. You are called to behold His glory, which you do through the Word. As you lift the Scriptures to the Spirit, He will reveal Himself more and more!

I encourage you to let these verses from Ephesians 1:15–23 and 2 Corinthians 3:18 (AMPC) be your prayer:

> "Therefore I...{pray} that the God of {my} Lord Jesus Christ, the Father of glory, may give to {me} the spirit of wisdom and revelation in the knowledge of Him, the eyes of {my} understanding being enlightened; that {I} may know what is the hope of His calling, what are the riches of the glory of His inheritance in the saints, and what is the exceeding greatness of His power toward us who believe, according to the working of His mighty power which He worked in Christ when He raised Him from the dead

and seated Him at His right hand in the heavenly places, far above all principality and power and might and dominion, and every name that is named, not only in this age but also in that which is to come. And He put all things under His feet, and gave Him to be head over all things to the church, which is His body, the fullness of Him who fills all in all."...

"And {I}, as with unveiled face, [because {I}] continued to behold [in the Word of God] as in a mirror the glory of the Lord, are constantly being transfigured into His very own image in ever increasing splendor and from one degree of glory to another; [for this comes] from the Lord [Who is] the Spirit."

Absolutely depend upon and trust God. He desires to take you from one degree of glory to the next.

Consider again what 2 Corinthians 3:18 says—that we are being transformed "...in ever increasing splendor and from one degree of glory to another; [for this comes] from the Lord [Who is] the Spirit." The Lord, who is the Spirit, causes you to increase from one degree of knowing Him to the next degree of splendor. Nothing you can do or say can bring you closer. That happens only by His invitation. The great news is that if you are a child of God, you have been invited and are continually being invited!

We cannot live off of yesterday's manna. We cannot replicate yesterday's glory and anointing. We must be endowed with the fresh oil and presence of Christ speaking and revealing Himself to us now!

When the children of Israel were in the wilderness, they had to follow the cloud of God's glory by day and the pillar of His fire by night. God had to teach them to be a people of His presence. Where the presence moved, they moved; where the presence camped, they camped. Finally, the resting place of God's glory was in the temple, and then it was tabernacled within Christ, the living and greater temple.

Today His glory and fire live in a new tabernacle: your body. You are the dwelling place of God, and His glory resides in you by the Holy Spirit. Great is the mystery, hidden from ages and generations, which is Christ in you, the hope of glory! (See Colossians 1:26–27.) The same God, the same One who invites us, wants to move and camp and lead you from one degree of glory to the next! Hallelujah!

Again, nothing you can do or say can cause you to move closer; it is only by His Spirit. This reality demands two very important responses from you: humility and dependence—humility because you are sustained by God alone, and dependence because it is the Lord who takes you from one degree of fullness to the next. He holds you and moves you. You just need to rely on His grace, strength, and power. You must learn to embrace your weakness before God so you can depend on Him in everything; that is where the power really rests, as we see in the following passages.

> And He said to me, "My grace is sufficient for you, for My strength is made perfect in weakness." Therefore most gladly I will rather boast in my infirmities, that the power of Christ may rest upon me. Therefore I take pleasure in infirmities, in reproaches, in needs, in persecutions, in distresses, for Christ's sake. For when I am weak, then I am strong.
>
> —2 CORINTHIANS 12:9–10

> And I, brethren, when I came to you, did not come with excellence of speech or of wisdom declaring to you the testimony of God. For I determined not to know anything among you except Jesus Christ and Him crucified. I was with you in weakness, in fear, and in much trembling. And my speech and my preaching were not with persuasive words of human wisdom, but in demonstration of the Spirit and of power, that your faith should not be in the wisdom of men but in the power of God.
>
> —1 CORINTHIANS 2:1–5

The secret of God's presence and power is absolute humility and dependence upon God Himself, not our own abilities or strengths. He can be trusted to take you from glory to glory!

CLOSING SCRIPTURES AND PRAYER

Here are some scriptures to enliven your spirit. These are some of my favorite passages to meditate on. May these scriptures enliven your heart as well! May you see them as prophetic exhortations straight from the Word of God. May they serve you in seeing the Lord of glory and yourself rightly. Pray and meditate on them with me.

> On the last day, that great day of the feast, Jesus stood and cried out, saying, "If anyone thirsts, let him come to Me and drink. He who believes in Me, as the Scripture has said, out of his heart will flow rivers of living water."
> —JOHN 7:37–38

> And the Spirit and the bride say, "Come!" And let him who hears say, "Come!" And let him who thirsts come. Whoever desires, let him take the water of life freely.
> —REVELATION 22:17

> For this reason I bow my knees to the Father of our Lord Jesus Christ, from whom the whole family in heaven and earth is named, that He would grant you, according to the riches of His glory, to be strengthened with

might through His Spirit in the inner man, that Christ may dwell in your hearts through faith; that you, being rooted and grounded in love, may be able to comprehend with all the saints what is the width and length and depth and height—to know the love of Christ which passes knowledge; that you may be filled with all the fullness of God. Now to Him who is able to do exceedingly abundantly above all that we ask or think, according to the power that works in us, to Him be glory in the church by Christ Jesus to all generations, forever and ever. Amen.

—Ephesians 3:14–21

Therefore I also, after I heard of your faith in the Lord Jesus and your love for all the saints, do not cease to give thanks for you, making mention of you in my prayers: that the God of our Lord Jesus Christ, the Father of glory, may give to you the spirit of wisdom and revelation in the knowledge of Him, the eyes of your understanding being enlightened; that you may know what is the hope of His calling, what are the riches of the glory of His inheritance in the saints, and what is the exceeding greatness of His power toward us who believe, according to the working of His mighty power which He worked in Christ when He raised Him from the dead and seated Him at His right hand in the heavenly places, far above all principality and power and might and dominion, and every name that is named, not only in this age but also in that which is to come. And He put all things under His feet, and gave Him to be head over all things to the church, which is His body, the fullness of Him who fills all in all.

—EPHESIANS 1:15–23

MY PRAYER FOR YOU!

May the Spirit of God fill you with ever-increasing glory and splendor. May you be filled with the fullness of God's Spirit, bringing you into the overflow of His peace and grace. May the love of God, the grace and peace from Christ, and the sweet abiding communion of the Holy Spirit be with your spirit. May you grow to love the Father, the living Word, and the Spirit. May the grace of Christ unveil the spirit of revelation and fill your heart with the divine light that proceeds from knowing Him.

May God keep you, strengthen you, and enlarge your capacity to receive more and more of Him. May you get out of the way and go low in humility so the King can come in and lift you into the heights to be seated with Him in heavenly places. May you and God share the same space; may you share in the thoughts and feelings of His heart. And may you become a light to a dark world. May you be filled with new wine and learn that waiting is your weapon against the flesh. May your spirit be strong and your flesh subdued by your spirit, and may your soul receive all the effects of being with Him. In Jesus' name, amen!

COMMON QUESTIONS
ABOUT WAITING
ON THE LORD

**Is waiting on the Lord something we do all day
long or just in our quiet time?**

Waiting on the Lord is a lifestyle. It can be done
in your intentional quiet time and throughout your
day. Don't put God in a formulaic box. Just learn to
wait on Him.

What does being renewed in strength look like?

Renewed strength is a grace we receive. It is spiritual. It is receiving spiritual vitality for your life.
To be renewed is to have peace; joy; the fruit of the
Spirit; strength, passion, and vigor for God; and the
ability to function without fatigue but from a place
of spiritual rest.

Is it wrong to be in silence through the entire prayer time?

Not at all. When I spend time with the Lord, I spend most of the time in silence and worship. There are times when God wants you to be still. The important thing is that the Spirit is leading you. God doesn't want us to make our time with Him into a formula. He's relational.

How long do you spend waiting each day?

The duration of time does not matter. It's not about the *quantity* of time but the *quality* of time. Some of the most powerful moments I've had with the Lord were five or fifteen minutes. Don't put yourself on a religious schedule that is impossible to keep. That will lead to a cycle of guilt when you don't fulfill your intended tasks. Don't treat the Lord like an item on a to-do list. Don't treat yourself like a taskmaster. The Lord doesn't want to be a chore but someone you love and cherish. So get quiet and begin praising the Lord. Don't worry about what to do. Just be with Him. Paul speaks of this wonderful reality in Romans 8:26: "Likewise the Spirit also helps in our weaknesses. For we do not know what we should pray for as we ought, but the Spirit Himself makes intercession for us with groanings which cannot be uttered." You don't have to know what to do or say—just be with Him.

Should I play worship music during my alone time?

Every person is different. When I spend time alone with Jesus, I don't really listen to anything because I've trained myself to be still, but there's nothing wrong with listening to worship music in your alone time. There is no one right way to do this. The goal is to connect with the Lord. If you want to use worship music to do that, then play worship music. If you want to connect with the Lord in silence, then sit in silence. The aim of your fellowship with the Lord is *connection* and communing with Him. As I've said before, don't put Him in a box. There have been many times when I was just silent with nothing playing. At other times, playing music helped me get quiet before Him. You're trying to be still in your spirit, not in your ears. Do what helps *you* to be still and get your mind and heart quiet.

What if I feel a tug to separate myself but have many distractions (such as my children or spouse)?

Even if your life is full and you have many distractions, you need to carve out time. It may be late at night or early in the morning, but you must carve out time, even if it's just a little bit. Make time for Him, and God will do the rest.

I'm a new mom. Should I feel bad if I can't wait longer than a minute or two?

Give yourself grace. God knows what's going on in your life. In the midst of all the chaos, begin to worship the Lord. Bring your little one to Him. He loves you, and He loves your little one. What you need to do is give yourself grace as God gives you grace.

How do I deal with random thoughts that pop up?

If you're worshipping and all of a sudden think, "I've got to fold laundry," and then another thought hits your head, open your mouth and begin to praise the Lord. As you do that, you will focus your mind on Him. The more you spend time with God and practice being still, the less often those thoughts will pop up. Being still before the Lord is often hard at first because it's not something we're used to doing. But if random thoughts pop into your head a million times, magnify the Lord a million times. Each time you do, you reorient yourself to the presence of God. Keep on putting your attention on the Holy Spirit, no matter how many times you need to do it.

How do I know if I'm battling a stronghold in my mind or soul?

If the imagination or thought contradicts the exalted Christ, then it is a stronghold and it needs to be torn down. *How do you do that?* By lifting the Lord Jesus, losing sight of yourself, getting into the Word of God, and believing what it says. If you think you need to tear down a stronghold, I encourage you to read Romans through Jude. Feast on that portion of Scripture until you get a revelation of your identity in Christ. We often magnify the wrong thing. Who cares if it's a demon? I know that may sound crazy, but if you cast your cares on *Christ*, the Lord will take care of the rest. Don't give the devil a foothold. Don't give him any free space to live in your mind. Do not be distracted by devils. Focus on Christ. Begin to exalt the Lord Jesus. The enemy doesn't like the presence of God. As you fill your mind with Him, He will do a great work.

NOTES

CHAPTER 2

1. Blue Letter Bible, s.v. "*sōma*," accessed April 20, 2024, https://www.blueletterbible.org/lexicon/g4983/kjv/tr/0-1/.
2. Blue Letter Bible, s.v. "*koilia*," accessed June 24, 2024, https://www.blueletterbible.org/lexicon/g2836/kjv/tr/0-1/.
3. Blue Letter Bible, s.v. "*rûaḥ*," accessed June 24, 2024, https://www.blueletterbible.org/lexicon/h7307/kjv/wlc/0-1/.
4. Blue Letter Bible, s.v. "*pneuma*," accessed June 24, 2024, https://www.blueletterbible.org/lexicon/g4151/kjv/tr/0-1/.
5. Blue Letter Bible, s.v. "*nep̄eš*," accessed June 26, 2024, https://www.blueletterbible.org/lexicon/h5315/kjv/wlc/0-1/.
6. Blue Letter Bible, s.v. "*rûaḥ*."
7. Blue Letter Bible, s.v. "*nešāmâ*," accessed July 2, 2024, https://www.blueletterbible.org/lexicon/h5397/kjv/wlc/0-1/.
8. Blue Letter Bible, s.v. "*logos*," accessed June 24, 2024, https://www.blueletterbible.org/lexicon/g3056/kjv/tr/0-2/#lexResults.
9. Blue Letter Bible, s.v. "*graphē*," accessed June 24, 2024, https://www.blueletterbible.org/lexicon/g1124/kjv/tr/0-1/.

10. Blue Letter Bible, s.v. "*nāṣar*," accessed June 24,2024, https://www.blueletterbible.org/lexicon/h5341/kjv/wlc/0-1/.

11. A. W. Tozer, *The Pursuit of God* (Harrisburg, PA: Christian Publications, 1948), chapter 7.

CHAPTER 3

1. Blue Letter Bible, s.v. "*kathairō*," accessed June 24, 2024, https://www.blueletterbible.org/lexicon/g2508/kjv/tr/0-1/.

2. Blue Letter Bible, s.v. "*hāgâ*," accessed June 24, 2024, https://www.blueletterbible.org/lexicon/h1897/kjv/wlc/0-1/.

3. Eric Gilmour (@sonshipintl), "Quietness is the absence of external noise but stillness is the absence of internal noise," Instagram photo, June 5, 2023, https://www.instagram.com/sonshipintl/p/CtG-incueae/.

4. Sruthi M., "Is It True Weight Loss is 80% Diet and 20% Exercise?," MedicineNet, accessed June 25, 2024, https://www.medicinenet.com/is_it_true_weight_loss_is_80_diet_and_20_exercise/article.htm.

5. StudyLight.org, s.v. "*hāgâ*," accessed June 24, 2024, https://www.studylight.org/lexicons/eng/hebrew/01897.html.

6. Bible Hub, s.v. "*hegeh*," accessed June 24, 2024, https://biblehub.com/bdb/1899.htm; Bible Hub, s.v. "*higgayon*," accessed June 24, 2024, https://biblehub.com/hebrew/1902.htm.

CHAPTER 4

1. Blue Letter Bible, s.v. "ʿôlām," accessed June 24, 2024, https://www.blueletterbible.org/lexicon/h5769/kjv/wlc/0-1/.
2. *Merriam-Webster*, s.v. "power," accessed June 25, 2024, https://www.merriam-webster.com/dictionary/power.
3. Blue Letter Bible, s.v. "qāvâ," accessed June 24, 2024, https://www.blueletterbible.org/lexicon/h6960/kjv/wlc/0-1/.
4. Blue Letter Bible, s.v. "qāvâ."
5. *Merriam-Webster*, s.v. "linger," accessed June 24, 2024, https://www.merriam-webster.com/dictionary/linger.

CHAPTER 5

1. *Oxford Languages*, s.v. "harmony," accessed April 26, 2024, https://www.google.com/search?q=harmony.
2. *Oxford Languages*, s.v. "communion," accessed April 26, 2024, https://www.google.com/search?q=communion.
3. *Oxford Languages*, s.v. "relationship," accessed April 26, 2024, https://www.google.com/search?q=relationship.
4. Charles Spurgeon (@_CSpurgeon_), "When asked, 'What is more important: Prayer or Reading the Bible,'" X, December 17, 2022, 3:01 p.m., https://twitter.com/_CSpurgeon_/status/1604205145763495936?lang=en.

CHAPTER 6

1. Blue Letter Bible, s.v. *"apokalypsis,"* accessed May 6, 2024, https://www.blueletterbible.org/lexicon/g602/kjv/tr/0-1/.
2. Blue Letter Bible, s.v. *"epignōsis,"* accessed May 6, 2024, https://www.blueletterbible.org/lexicon/g1922/kjv/tr/0-1/.
3. Bible Hub, s.v. *"epignósis,"* accessed June 24, 2024, https://biblehub.com/greek/1922.htm.

CHAPTER 7

1. Robert Bratcher, "The Meaning of Kosmos, 'World', in the New Testament," *The Bible Translator* 31, no. 4 (October 1980): 430, https://doi.org/10.1177/026009438003100406.
2. Blue Letter Bible, s.v. *"pānîm,"* accessed June 24, 2024, https://www.blueletterbible.org/lexicon/h6440/kjv/wlc/0-5/#lexResults.

CHAPTER 8

1. Blue Letter Bible, s.v. *"monogenēs,"* accessed June 24, 2024, https://www.blueletterbible.org/lexicon/g3439/kjv/tr/0-1/.
2. Dovid Rosenfeld, "Isaac's Age at the Binding (Akeidah)," Aish, accessed June 26, 2024, https://aish.com/isaacs-age-at-the-binding-akeidah/; Larry White, "How Old Was Jesus When He Died?" Bible Study Tools, updated April 13, 2022, https://www.biblestudytools.com/bible-study/topical-studies/how-old-was-jesus-when-he-died.html.

3. Blue Letter Bible, s.v. "Lead, Led," accessed June 24, 2024, https://www.blueletterbible.org/search/Dictionary/viewTopic.cfm?topic=VT0001622.

CONCLUSION

1. *Merriam-Webster*, s.v. "mirror," accessed May 4, 2024, https://www.merriam-webster.com/dictionary/mirror.

ABOUT THE AUTHOR

CHRIS GARCIA IS the founder of Father's Glory International and the senior overseer at House of Glory in Fort Smith, Arkansas. Chris is a revivalist at heart and longs to see the fullness of the presence and power of God in the local church and abroad. Chris is best known for his thriving YouTube channel and his program *Fresh Oil*, which is live streamed on YouTube to help people foster greater intimacy with the Holy Spirit by learning how to spend time with God.

Chris travels regionally and internationally to aid the local church in cultivating a greater awareness of God's glory. He also hosts annual events called The Fresh Oil Outpouring, which are regional gatherings that focus on worship, prayer, and impartation.

Chris is a lover of prayer and meditation on God's Word. It is the theme of his life to bring the local church to a greater awareness of God's glory in their personal and corporate lives.

To connect with Chris, visit:

Chris's YouTube channel:
www.youtube.com/@ChrisGarcia.

Father's Glory International:
www.fathersglory.org

House of Glory:
www.thehouseofglory.org